D0978879

THE BOOK OF OUTDOOR KNOTS

For Charlie Owen

· THE BOOK OF ·
OUTDOOR KNOTS

PETER OWEN

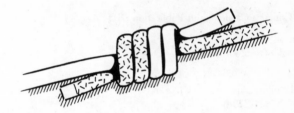

LYONS & BURFORD, PUBLISHERS

Design by Peter Owen.

Printed in the United States of America

10 9 8 7 6 5 4 3 2 1

Library of Congress Cataloging-in-Publication Data

Owen, Peter, 1955-
    The book of outdoor knots / Peter Owen.
        p. cm.
    Includes bibliographical references and index.
    ISBN 1-55821-225-6

    1. Knots and splices.   I. Title
VM533.094 1993
623.88'82–dc20

93-9112
CIP

CONTENTS

INTRODUCTION

A knot is a connection in a line, cord, or piece of rope, and can be in the line itself, between two lines, or the means by which something is attached to a line. It is made by passing the working end (the free end) of a line through a loop and pulling it tight or by tying different lines, cords, or lengths of rope together. Learning how to form a knot properly and knowing which knot to use for a given purpose is essential to the safety and enjoyment of many outdoor pursuits – and could mean the difference between life and death.

There are several distinct groups of knots, each of which is used for different purposes: stopper knots, running knots, loops, hitches, and bends, as well as fishing knots used to connect thin lines. Within each group there are many variations, but it is not necessary to know every one; four or five should be sufficient. The most important thing is selecting the right knot for the job and being able to tie it quickly and properly, whatever the conditions.

Finally, you should remember that knots reduce the breaking strain of any line, whatever the material, by between five to twenty percent. Knots slip just before they break, but if a knot is correctly tied and drawn as tight as possible, it will withstand a much greater strain before it begins to slip.

ROPE MANUFACTURE

Traditionally, rope was made by twisting fibers of natural materials together. The fibers were twisted first into yarn, then into strands, and finally into rope, in a process called laying up. If you examine a piece of ordinary three-strand rope you will notice the strands go up and to the right. It has been "laid" right-handed. When the rope was made the fibers were twisted together to form right-hand yarn, the yarn was then twisted in the opposite direction to form left-hand strands, and these were twisted to form right-laid rope. If you uncoil one strand you can clearly see it is laid up left-handed, or twisted the opposite way to the whole rope. This is the vital principle of traditional rope making. Even with one strand removed the other two strands cling together, leaving a groove where the missing strand should be. It is this alternate twisting that creates the tension that holds the rope together and gives it strength.

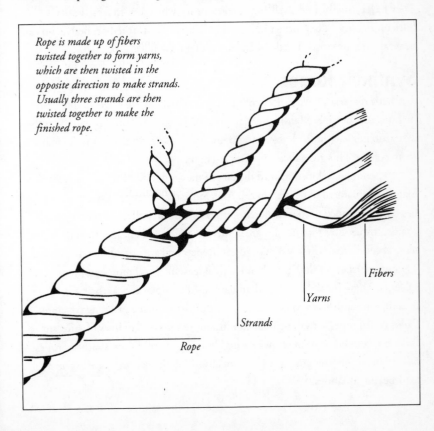

Rope is made up of fibers twisted together to form yarns, which are then twisted in the opposite direction to make strands. Usually three strands are then twisted together to make the finished rope.

Fibers

Yarns

Strands

Rope

Natural Fiber Ropes

For thousands of years, until shortages during the Second World War led to the development of man-made fibers, rope was made from natural materials – cotton and flax for manageability, coir and sisal for cheapness, manila and hemp for strength.

Natural fiber rope is normally three-strand and right laid. Four-strand, left-laid rope is much rarer and ten percent weaker – adding further strands does not increase strength. Cable-laid line (a nine-strand cable laid up left-handed from three three-strand ropes) is forty percent weaker than hawser-laid (three-strand) rope of the same diameter.

Natural fibers are only as long as the plant from which they were derived allows; the ends of these individual fibers (known as staples) are what gives natural rope its hairy, rough appearance. This gives them better traction and resistance than smooth man-made fibers. However, natural fibers have many disadvantages. They lack elasticity, and swell and become heavy when wet, making knots difficult to untie. They attract mildew and will rot if not stored properly, and can be weakened and made brittle by strong sunlight, chemicals, and salt.

Synthetic Ropes

Synthetic materials have almost completely replaced natural fibers in the manufacture of rope. Man-made filaments can be spun to run the whole length of a line, do not vary in thickness, and do not have to be twisted together to make them cohere. This gives them superior strength.

Nylon, developed toward the end of the Second World War, was the first man-made material to be used in this way. Since then a range of synthetic ropes has been developed to meet different purposes, but they all share certain characteristics. Size for size they are lighter, stronger, and cheaper than their natural counterparts. They do not rot or mildew and are not affected by sea water. They are resistant to sunlight, chemicals, oil, gasoline, and most common solvents. They absorb less water than natural-fiber ropes, and so their wet breaking strength remains constant. They can also be made in a range of colors. Color coded ropes for sailing make for instant recognition of lines of different function; colored climbing ropes are highly visible. In addition, synthetic ropes have high tensile strength, are capable of absorbing shocks, and have excellent load-bearing qualities.

BRAIDED ROPE

The combination of an outer sheath surrounding an inner core makes braided rope, softer, more flexible and quite a lot stronger than other types of synthetic rope.

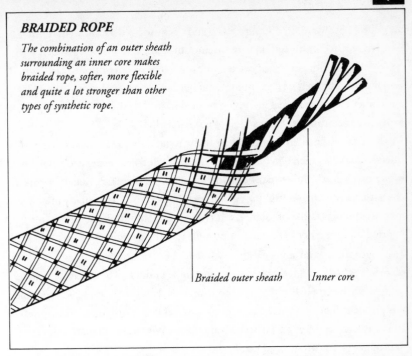

Braided outer sheath   Inner core

Nylon (Polyamide) fibers make ropes that are both strong and elastic, giving them an outstanding capacity for absorbing shock loads. They are good for towing and, because they do not rot or float, they are particularly useful in sailing. Nylon fibers, slightly modified chemically, are used in climbing rope. They are also used in fishing line, which has to be tough, flexible, and easily knotted, and must hold knots well.

Polyester ropes are nearly as strong as nylon and give very little stretch. They do not float and are highly resistant to wear and weathering. They are widely used in sailing for sheets and halyards. Polyester is also used in small sizes for twine.

Polypropylene is not as strong as nylon or polyester but it makes a good, inexpensive, all-purpose rope. It is highly resistant to weather, light, and the kind of hydrocarbon pollution found on the surfaces of harbors with substantial motor boat traffic. It is the only fiber that floats well, and thus is particularly suitable for water-ski tow ropes, rescue lines, and large ship moorings. Floating does mean, however, that it may be caught in or cut by a propeller.

Rope made from polyethylene is weaker than other synthetic rope. It is very cheap, but stretches and slips easily and does not hold a knot well. It is not widely used, except for certain very specific purposes, and it is best avoided.

Aramid fibers are the newest and strongest to be developed so far. Aramid is light, does not melt (it decomposes at about 500 degrees Centigrade or 932 Fahrenheit) and has a breaking strength equal to steel. It is, however, very expensive and sensitive to the action of ultraviolet light.

One of the disadvantages of synthetic ropes, other than those of aramid fibers, is that they melt when heated. Even the friction heat generated when one rope rubs against another may be enough to cause damage. It is vital, therefore, to check that ropes are not rubbing against each other; this is particularly important for rock climbers and mountaineers. It is also possible for heat friction to fuse knotted rope together so that it is impossible to untie the knot.

Another disadvantage is that synthetic ropes made of continuous filaments are so smooth that knots slip and come undone. Knots may need to be secured by an extra half-hitch, and some ropes are laid up in the old way to avoid this problem. The filaments are chopped into lengths, to give the rope hairiness and resistance to slippage. Then the filaments are twisted in alternative directions to produce yarns, strands and finally laid-up rope.

The other types of synthetic rope are plaited or braided. Plaited describes four- or eight-stranded solid plaits. Braided rope has an outer sheath of sixteen or more strands surrounding a core that is either braided and hollow or made up of solid parallel, or slightly twisted, filaments. Braided rope is softer, more flexible, and quite a lot stronger. It is very much favored by mountaineers.

A rope twice the diameter of another (everything else being equal) has four times the strength. Choice should not be made, however, on strength alone. If the rope is to take shock loads then elasticity may be more important; in that case a polyester polyamide would be the best rope to select.

Laid-up rope, made of thick multifilaments tightly twisted together, may be very resistant to wear but it may also be difficult to tie and knots may not hold well. Do not buy a rope that is too stiff. It will not, whatever the salesperson tells you, get more supple with time. Similarly, be wary of twisted rope that is very soft.

Sailors should use a rope that floats only for rescue work, light buoys, etc. Floating lines should not be used for anchorage in ports as they risk immediate severing by the propellers of motorboats.

CHOOSING AND CARING FOR ROPE

Choose a rope according to what it will be used for, the material it is made of, and the type (i.e. braided or laid up).

	Nylon	Polyester	Polypropylene
General Outdoor Use	●		
Climbing	●		
Anchorage	●	●	
Mooring	●	●	●
Rigging		●	
Towing	●		●
Fishing	●		

Sealing Ends

When you buy synthetic rope from a chandlery or dealer, they will cut it to the length you require with an electrically heated knife. This seals the ends and gives a sharp edge. When you cut synthetic rope yourself, use a sharp knife and then melt the end with a cigarette lighter. Smooth and round off the clean melt with a moistened finger. Always seal in this way, and repair fraying ends by sealing or whipping, or you will lose yards of useful rope.

Looking After Rope

Rope is sturdy material, but it is expensive, so it's worth looking after properly. Caring for rope will keep its strength and prolong its life. Avoid dragging it over rough, sharp edges, or dirty, gritty surfaces where particles could get into the rope and damage the fibers. Do not walk on rope or force it into harsh kinks. Inspect it regularly and wash off dirt, grit, and oil. Coil rope carefully and always make sure it is dry before coiling, even if it is synthetic. If it has been in sea water rinse thoroughly to remove all salt deposits. At the end of the season, wash all ropes in a mild detergent, removing oil or tar stains with gasoline or trichloroethylene.

Rope is weakened by tying knots in it. The tighter the nip and the sharper the curve the greater the chances that the rope will break; if it does it will part immediately outside the knot. Some of the most harmful knots are the most widely used – for example, the simple overhand knot (see pg. 16). Hitches, such as the clove hitch (see pg. 80) and fisherman's bend (see pg. 94), are gentler on rope as some of the load is absorbed by the friction in the turns.

Finally, never use two ropes of different materials together because only the more rigid of the two will work under the strain.

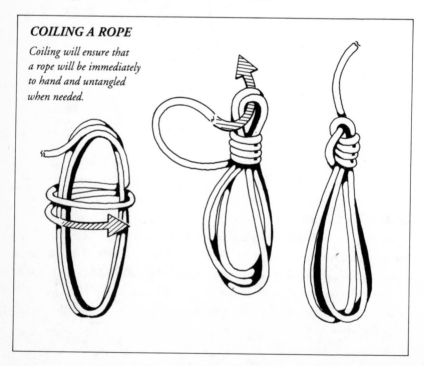

COILING A ROPE

Coiling will ensure that a rope will be immediately to hand and untangled when needed.

Selecting Knots

The main factor to consider when selecting one knot above another is the relative strength of the knots. This is particularly important for mountaineers and climbers, but knot strength is also something mariners need to take into consideration. Other factors influencing choice will be the speed and ease with which a knot can be tied, the size of the finished knot, and its reliability.

Climbers' knots tend to be bulky, with several wrapping turns to absorb the strain and prevent the rope from being weakened unnecessarily. It is very important for climbers to check their knots regularly, especially if the rope they are using is at all stiff. Stiff rope is more difficult to tie than very flexible line and the knots in it may be less secure.

Anglers' knots are similar to those used by climbers, but much smaller, and generally tied in thin, monofilament line. They also need the strength and reliability of wrapping turns if they are to secure their catch and not lose valuable tackle.

Select the right knot for the right job. Remember that knots perform differently under different sorts of strain. Some knots remain very strong while subjected to steady loading but will slip and even fall apart (capsize) if submitted to intermittent jerking. These knots, although strong, are insecure and should not be used in situations where they might come under sudden violent stress.

Being able to untie a knot is as important as knowing how to tie it. Usually knots should be untied after you have used them. This is made easier if you have chosen a suitable knot in the first place and tied it correctly. If you want to be able to untie a knot quickly, introduce a draw-loop. The knot will be no less strong and secure but it can be undone with a single tug. Knots like the clove hitch (see pg. 80) and the Prusik knot (see pg. 100) are efficient and reliable but disappear as soon as they are slipped off their foundation.

Finally, remember that mastering anything takes practice, and tying knots is no exception. The only way to learn how to tie a specific knot is in a relaxed atmosphere, not half-way up a mountain or out at sea in a storm. Practice knots over and over until the movements become automatic. Your own life, or the lives of others, may depend on it, so you must have the skill and confidence to be able to tie the knots you need correctly and without hesitation or doubt – no matter what the situation or how difficult the conditions.

How to use this book

The diagrams accompanying the descriptions of the knots are intended to be self-explanatory. There are arrows to show the directions in which you should push or pull the working ends of the rope or line. The dotted lines indicate intermediate positions of the rope. Always follow the order shown of going over or under a length of line; reversing or changing this order could result in a completely different knot which might well be unstable, unsafe, and insecure.

Rope Parts

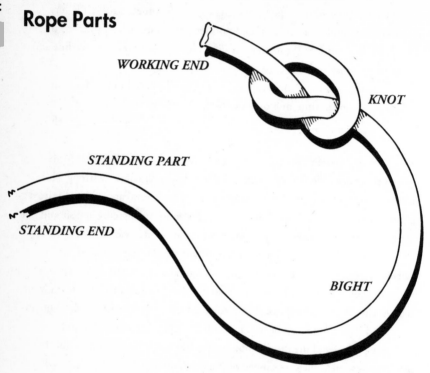

WORKING END

KNOT

STANDING PART

STANDING END

BIGHT

WARNING
Friction generated heat may cause synthetic rope to weaken and break without warning (see pg.10). Extreme caution, especially by rock climbers and mountaineers should be exercised when using synthetic rope in situations that may cause friction damage. The result could be fatal.

1
STOPPER KNOTS

Stopper knots, as their name suggests, are used to prevent the ends of a rope or line from slipping through an eye, loop, or hole. They can be used to bind the end of a line so that it will not unravel and can also be used decoratively. Stopper knots are used by climbers, campers, and fishermen. At sea they are used to weight lines and at the ends of running rigging.

The most important knot of this type is the overhand. This is the simplest, and perhaps the oldest, knot known to man and is used as the basis for countless others. Sailors tend to use the figure-eight stopper for general purposes and multiple overhand knots to weight the ends of ropes and for decoration.

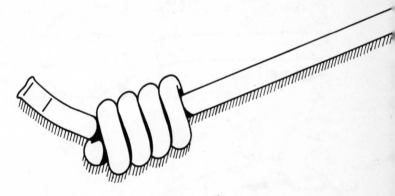

Heaving Line Knot

OVERHAND KNOT

Also known as the thumb knot, this knot forms the basis for many others. It is used in its own right as a stopper knot and is tied at regular intervals along life lines. Its most common application is probably to keep sewing thread from passing through the eye of a needle. It is not, however, popular with sailors as it is very difficult to untie when wet. Similarly, a tight overhand knot in small-diameter line is hard to undo.

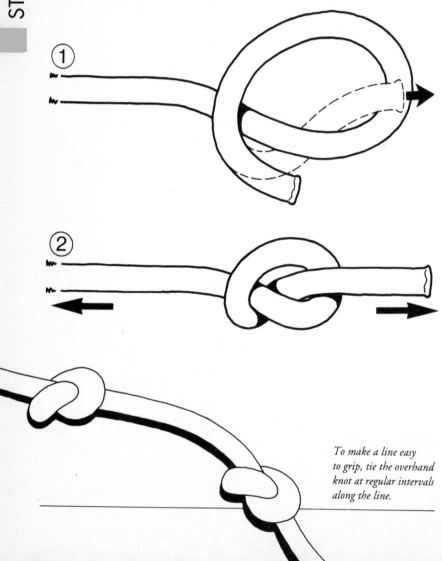

To make a line easy to grip, tie the overhand knot at regular intervals along the line.

FIGURE-EIGHT KNOT

The knot's name comes from its characteristic shape. It is the most important stopper knot for sailors, used on running rigging. (It is also known as the Flemish knot or Savoy knot).

The knot is made in the end of a line, with the upper loop around the standing part and the lower loop around the working end. Its interlaced appearance has long been seen as a symbol of interwoven affection. In heraldry it signifies faithful love and appears on various coats of arms – hence its other names.

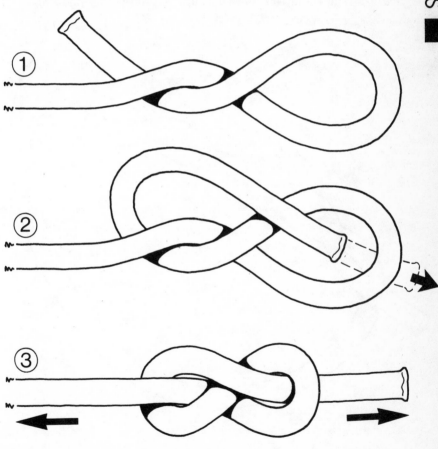

MULTIPLE OVERHAND KNOT

This knot, also known as the blood knot, earned its other name because it was the knot used to weight the ends of the lashes in the cat 'o nine tails, the whip used historically to flog soldiers, sailors, and criminals. It is also traditionally used by Capuchin friars to weight the cords on their habits and make them hang properly. Sailors use the knot as a weighting or a stopper on small-diameter line, although it becomes difficult to untie when the line is wet.

When tying the knot, keep the loop open and slack as you make the turns and then gently pull on both ends at the same time, twisting the two ends in opposite directions.

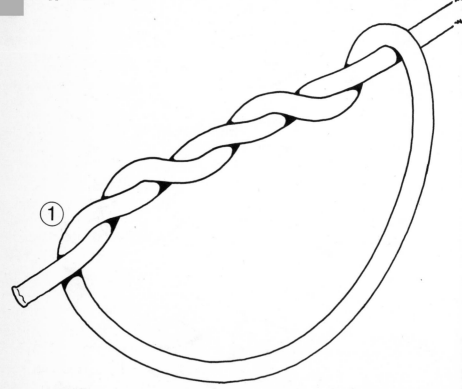

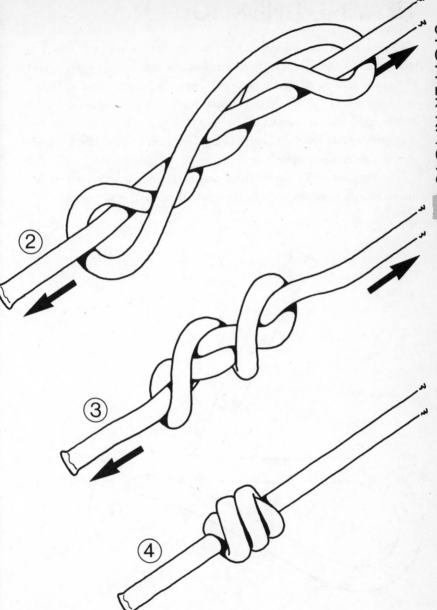

② ③ ④

HEAVING LINE KNOT

This knot is used in sailing when a heavy line is to be thrown from boat to shore or to another vessel. The heavy line is attached to a *heaving* line, a lighter line that is thrown across the gap first so the heavier line can be drawn behind it. The heaving line knot is tied in the end of this lighter line to give it weight and aid in throwing. Heaving lines are usually one-half to three-quarters of an inch in diameter and may be up to eighty feet long. They should float, be flexible, and be strong enough to bear a man's weight.

The knot's other names (Franciscan knot, monk's knot) derive from its use by Franciscan monks to weight the ends of the cords they use as belts.

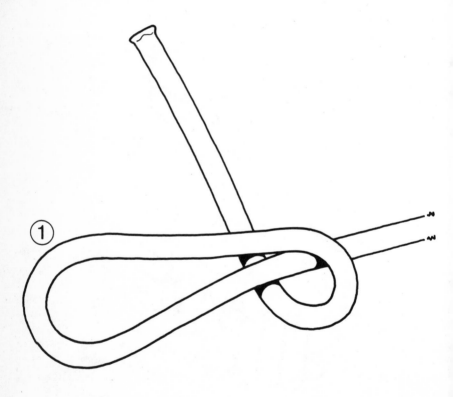

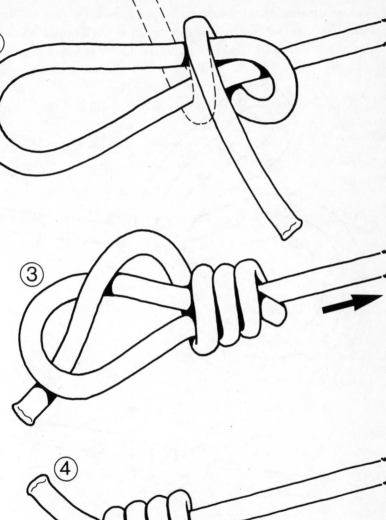

OVERHAND LOOP

This knot is useful if a stopper with more bulk is required. It is very difficult to untie, but it is the loop used instinctively by most people if they need to fasten a knot in the end of a piece of string and it does not have to be untied again.

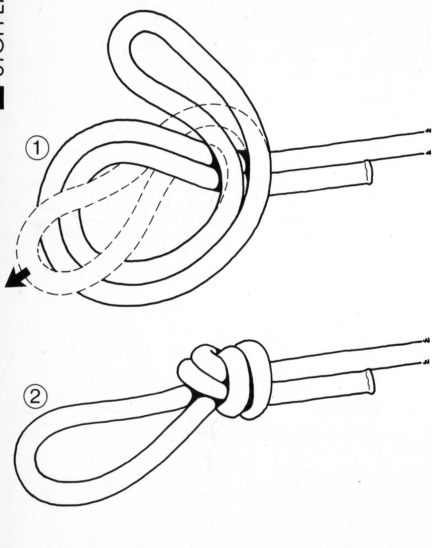

2
BENDS

Bends are used to join two lengths of rope at their ends to form one longer piece. It is important, if bends are to be secure, for the ropes joined in this way to be of the same kind and the same diameter. The sheet bend (pg. 28) is the exception to this rule. It is very secure, even when it is used to join ropes of different diameters.

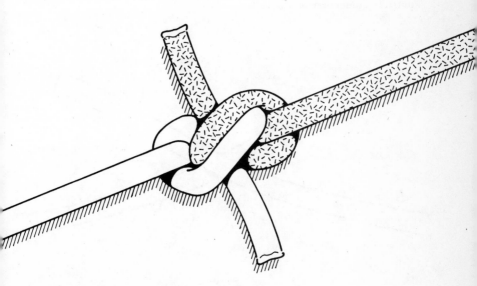

Hunter's Bend

REEF KNOT

The reef knot, or square knot, was known during the Late Stone Age and to the ancient Greeks and Romans. It gets its name from its nautical use to tie two ends of a rope when reefing a sail. It is very often the only knot many people know, apart from the granny knot. When the ends are only partly drawn through the knot, leaving loops, the resulting double reef bow is often used to tie shoe laces.

The reef knot is not a secure bend and should not be used as one, certainly never with ropes of different diameter. Its true function is to join together the ends of the same rope or string. It should *only* be used to make a temporary join in lines of identical type, weight, and diameter where it will not be put under strain. If the lines have to take strain, stopper knots should be tied in the short ends.

The knot is made up of two half knots. The first half knot starts left over right, the second is added right over left, and both short ends finish on the same side. If the knot is flat but the short ends are not on the same side, it is a thief knot. If the knot is raised and uneven it is a granny. Neither of these are secure knots and should be avoided.

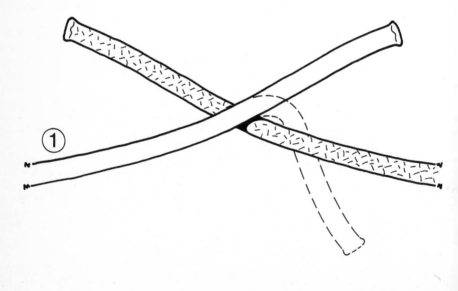

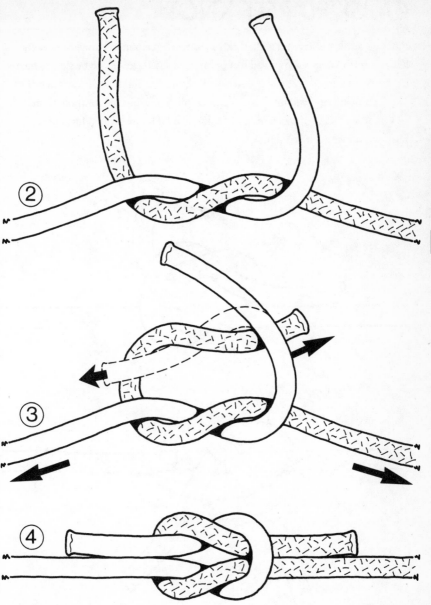

CAPSIZED REEF KNOT

Pulling sharply on one end will quickly capsize the reef knot. This version of the knot, also known as the capsized reef or capsized square knot, can be slipped apart easily. This makes it useful to sailors when reefing sails but it also means that the knot is unstable and will untie if one end is pulled or subjected to strain. Capsized reef knots have caused accidents and the knot should only be used for those purposes for which it is suited.

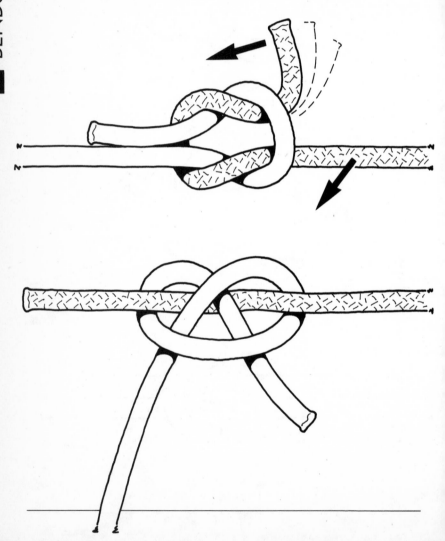

THIEF KNOT

The thief knot closely resembles the reef knot and, according to legend, it was used by whalers to tie their clothes bags. A thief would re-tie with a reef knot and the sailor would know his bag had been tampered with. The thief knot differs from the reef knot in the way it is tied and, in the finished knot, the short ends are on the opposite sides.

BENDS

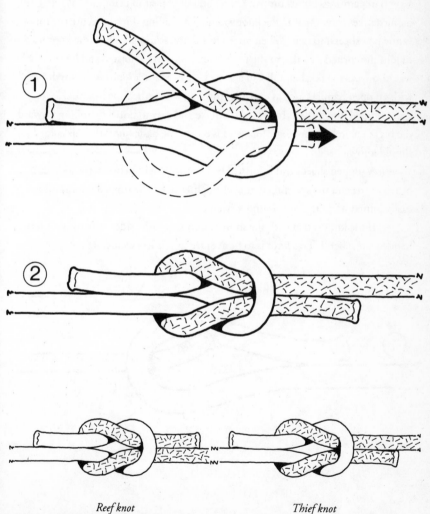

Reef knot   Thief knot

SHEET BEND

The sheet bend is probably the most commonly used of all bends and, unlike most other bends, it can safely join lines of different thickness. It is not, however, one hundred percent secure and should never be used in circumstances where it will be subjected to great strain. Its breaking strength also decreases in direct proportion to the difference in diameter of the lines joined.

The sheet bend (or common or flag bend) has been identified in ancient Egyptian paintings but its present name did not appear in print until 1794. The name derives from the way the knot was used on sailing ships to secure the ropes (known as sheets) to sails. When put to its other traditional use, as the knot used to join the corners of a flag to the rope when it was to be hoisted and lowered, it was known as the flag bend. It can also be used to make a rope fast to anything with an open handle (such as a spade), through which the rope is passed and then trapped under itself. It is quick to make and easy to untie, by rolling forward the bight encircling the single line, and is one of the basic knots that all sailors should know.

A slipped sheet bend is formed by placing a bight between the loop of the heavier rope and the standing part of the lighter one. The slipped knot is more easily untied when the rope is under strain.

If the knot is tied with the short ends on opposite sides, it becomes a left-handed sheet bend. This knot is to be avoided as it is less secure.

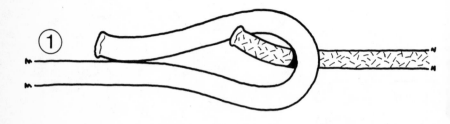

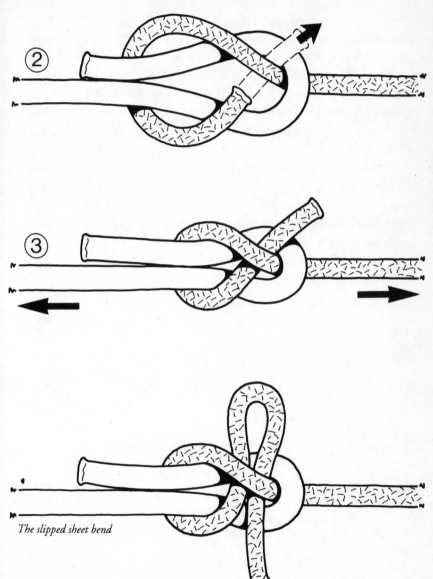

(2)

(3)

The slipped sheet bend

FISHERMAN'S KNOT

This knot is said to have been invented in the nineteenth century, but some authorities suggest it was known to the ancient Greeks. It is generally known as the fisherman's knot but over the years it has picked up many different names (such as angler's knot, English knot, Englishman's bend, halibut knot, true lover's bend and waterman's knot). It is formed from two overhand knots that jam against each other; the short ends are on opposite sides and lie almost parallel to their nearest standing part. After use, the two component knots are generally easily separated and undone.

The fisherman's knot should be used to join lines of equal thickness and is not suitable for large or medium diameter rope. It is not, therefore, often used by sailors. It is, however, well suited to string, cord, twine, or small stuff, and is widely used by anglers to join fishing line. The knot is not as strong as the line itself when under great strain.

NOTE: The fisherman's knot and the fisherman's bend are quite different and should not be confused with each other.

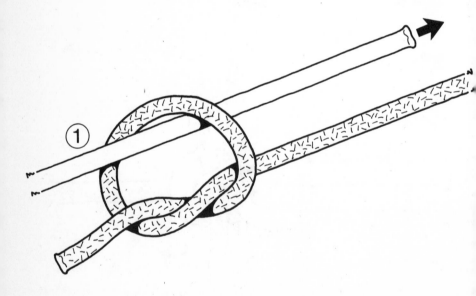

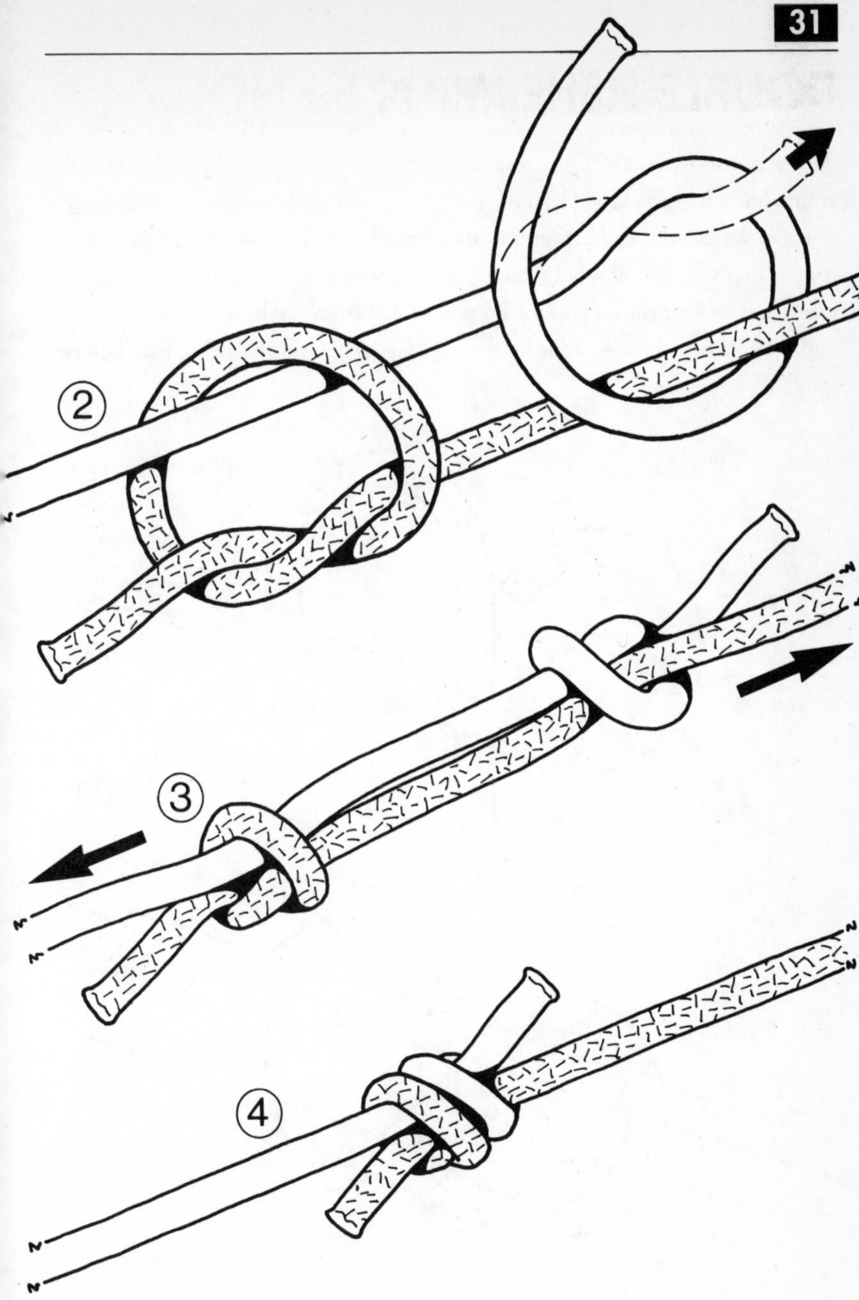
2
3
4

DOUBLE FISHERMAN'S KNOT

This very strong knot is commonly used, as the name suggests, by anglers to secure lines. It is also used by climbers and on small stuff, and campers use it on tent guy ropes and to join lengths of string needed to tie up or hang objects. It is quite a bulky knot so it is only suitable for use with thin lines and string. Climbers often tape or seize the ends of the knot to keep it from catching on the rock face and to minimize the risk of the knot's working loose. It is also called the grapevine knot.

BENDS

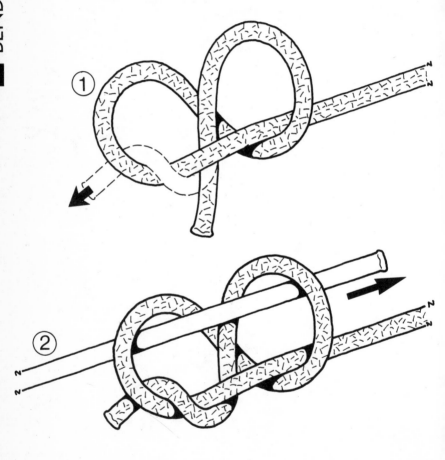

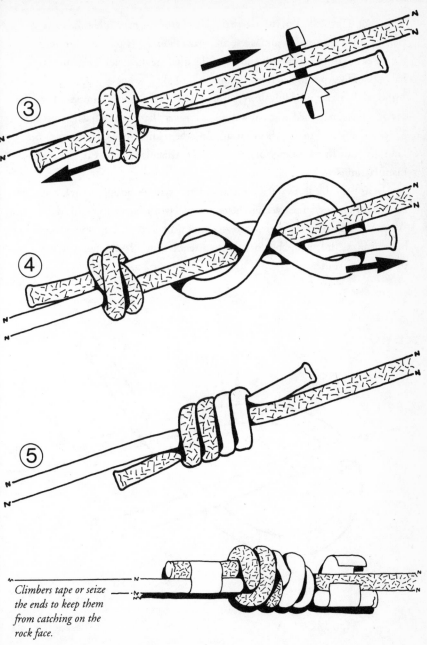

③

④

⑤

*Climbers tape or seize
the ends to keep them
from catching on the
rock face.*

CARRICK BEND

This knot is formed from two overhand knots crossing each other. It is a very stable knot, does not slip, and is a secure way of joining two ropes of similar diameter but different type. It can be used with large diameter ropes such as hawsers and warp ropes, and in climbing it is used to tie heavy ropes together. Although its name probably derives from a Medieval western European ship, the carrack, it is rarely used at sea nowadays as it is very hard to undo when wet or if it has been subjected to very heavy strain. Its other names (cowboy, split or warp knot) indicate its wide range of users – from cowhands to knitwear manufacturers.

In its flat form it is valued for its distinctive symmetric appearance. It can be used as a fastening on scarves and belts and is a favorite among graphic designers. When it is drawn up it capsizes into an entirely different shape; it is no less strong but this makes it less suitable for mountaineers as it may be too bulky to pass through a carabiner.

BENDS

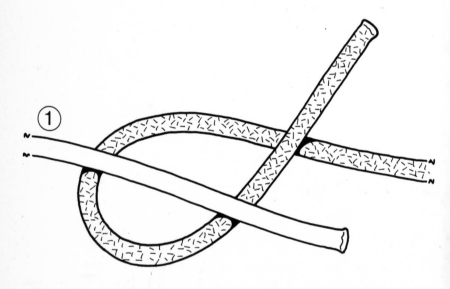

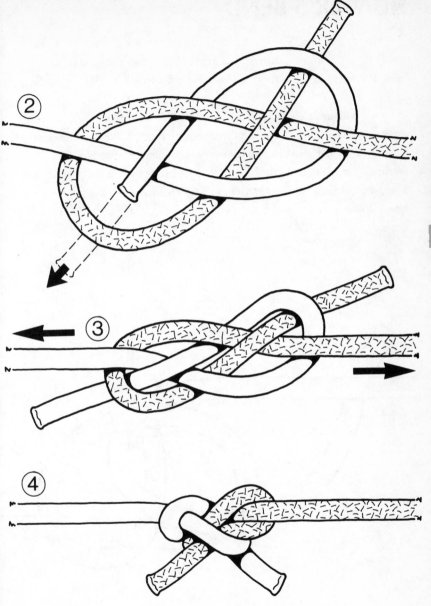

HUNTER'S BEND

The Hunter's or rigger's bend is based on two overhand knots. It is stable, has a good grip and is stronger than the fisherman's bend, the sheet bend or the reef knot. It is not as strong as the blood knot but it does have the advantage of being easy to untie.

It is named after Dr. Edward Hunter, a retired physician, who was reported to have invented it in 1968. Subsequent research, however, revealed that the same knot had been described nearly twenty years earlier by Phil D. Smith, in an American publication called 'Knots for Mountaineers.' He had devised the knot while working on the waterfront in San Francisco and called it the rigger's bend. Whoever first invented it, the Hunter's or rigger's bend remains a good general purpose knot with many useful qualities.

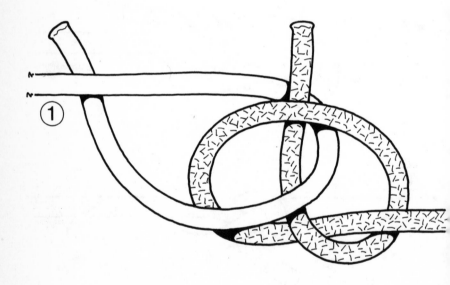

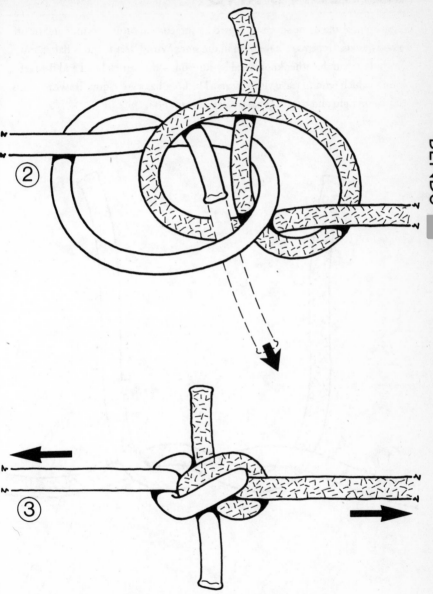

SURGEON'S KNOT

This knot, as the name suggests, is used by surgeons to suture wounds and tie off blood vessels. It seems to have been in use since World War II and is flatter and less bulky than the other knots used by surgeons – the carrick bend and the reef knot – which tend to leave visible scars. The knot has a good grip. It twists as it is drawn up tight and the diagonal is wrapped around it.

BENDS

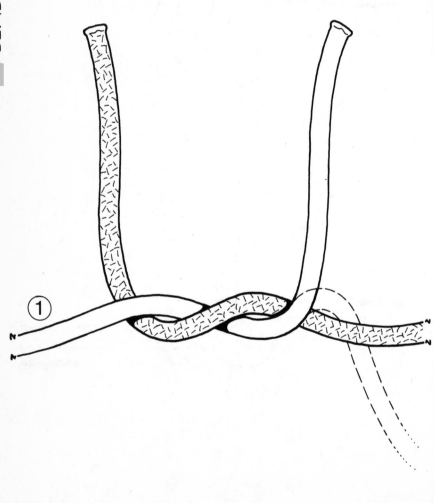

1

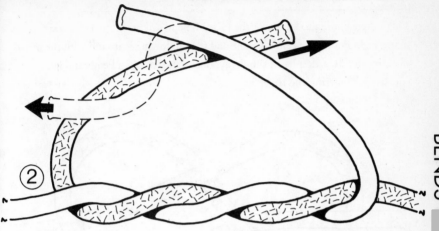

②

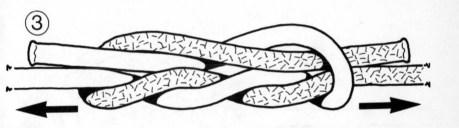

③

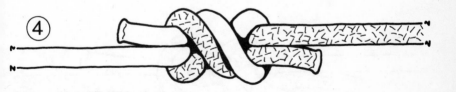

④

FIGURE-EIGHT BEND

This simple knot (also known as the Flemish bend or knot) is tied by making a figure-eight knot in one end of a line and then following it around with the other working end. It is, despite its simplicity, one of the strongest bends and holds equally well in string and rope.

BENDS

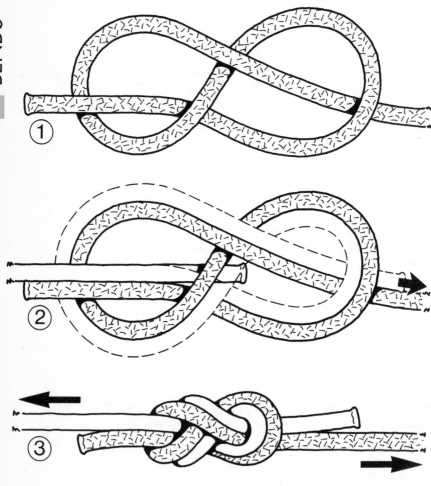

3
LOOPS

Knots made in the end of rope by folding it back into an eye or loop and then knotting it to its own standing part are called loops. They are fixed and do not slide. Unlike hitches, which are formed around an object and follow its shape, they are made in the hand to drop over an object. Loops are used widely by campers, climbers, and fishermen. They are particularly important to sailors who find these knots, especially the bowline, indispensable.

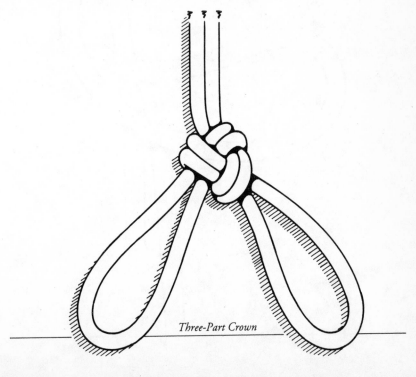

Three-Part Crown

FIGURE-EIGHT LOOP

This knot is comparatively easy to tie and stays tied, even when stiff rope is used. It has many applications and is often used by climbers to attach a line to a carabiner. Its unmistakable appearance makes it easy to check by a team leader. Its disadvantages – it is difficult to adjust and cannot easily be untied after loading – tend to be outweighed by its usefulness. It is also known as the figure-eight on the bight.

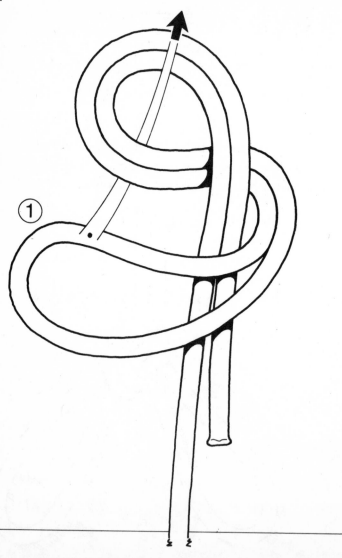

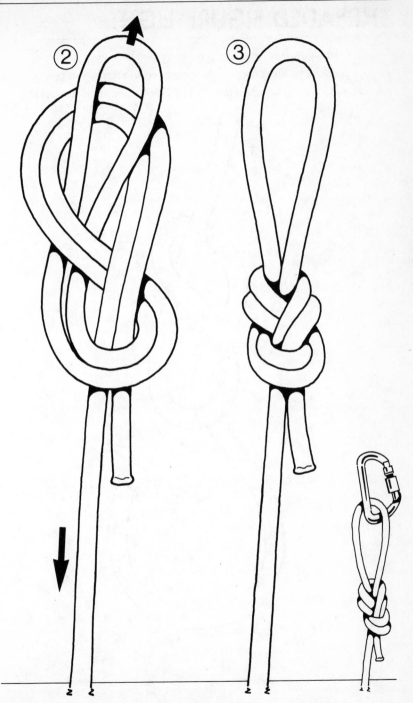

THREADED FIGURE-EIGHT

This variation of the figure-eight loop is widely used in climbing for tying on to the rope and for anchoring non-climbing members to a team. A stopper knot should be added when using the threaded figure-eight loop to tie on to a line.

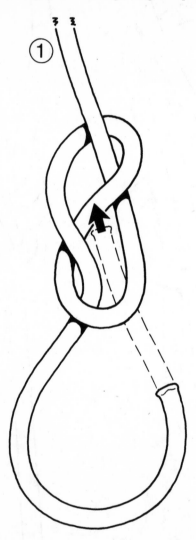

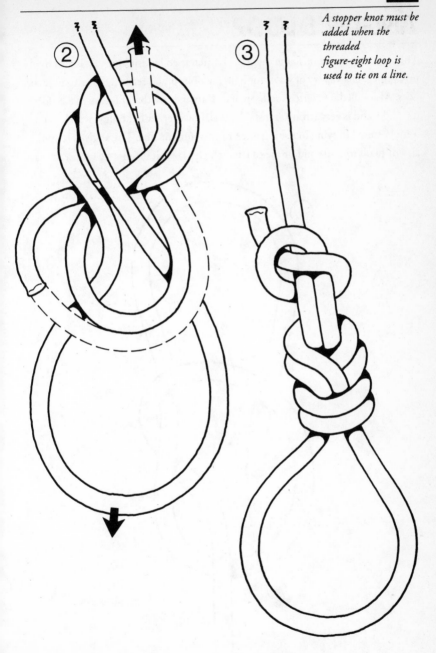

② ③

A stopper knot must be added when the threaded figure-eight loop is used to tie on a line.

ANGLER'S LOOP

The angler's loop, as its name suggests, is often used by fishermen. It is also used by campers in a variety of ways, for hanging objects and securing lines to poles or pegs. Also called the perfection loop, its advantages are that it is easy to tie, does not slide, and is very strong and stable. It is, however, rather bulky, which makes it more suited to tying in fishing line or fine synthetic line. The angler's loop is also difficult to untie and prone to jam, which makes it unsuitable for use at sea.

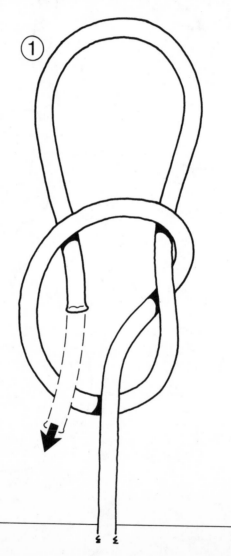

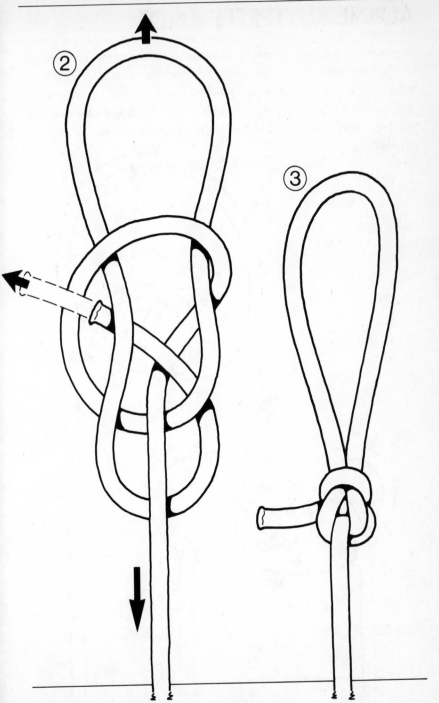

ALPINE BUTTERFLY KNOT

This knot is used by climbers and mountaineers. It fits around the chest and, because it is symmetrical, it holds equally well whichever end is held. It can be tied quickly, unties easily, does not slip and the loop does not shrink when the knot is tightened. Its major disadvantage is that it is difficult to tie; the increased use of the Italian hitch has meant that the alpine butterfly knot has lost some of its popularity.

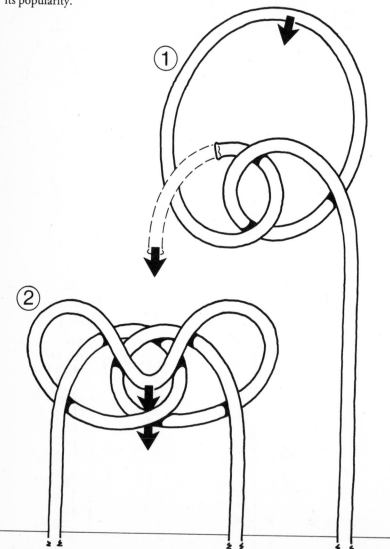

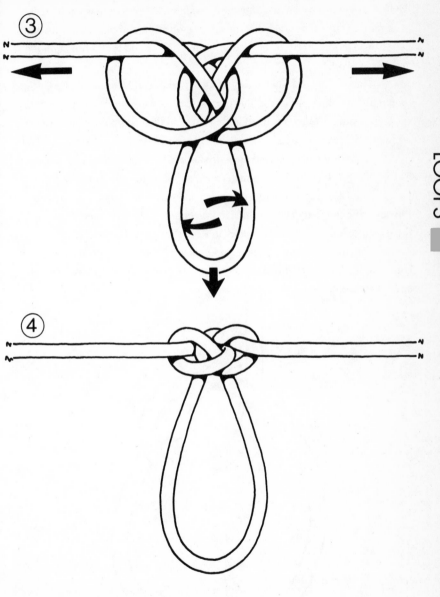

THE BOWLINE

The bowline is one of the best known and widely used knots and is particularly important to sailors. It is tied to form a fixed loop at the end of a line or to attach a rope to an object. At sea it is used on running rigging and for hoisting, joining, and salvage work.

The bowline is simple to tie, strong, and stable. It is formed by making a loop in the standing part of the line, passing the working end through the eye of the loop, around the back of the standing part and then down through the eye again. To be really safe finish the bowline off with a stopper knot or an extra half hitch to prevent it from turning into a slip knot.

The bowline's main advantages are that it does not slip, come loose, or jam. It is quick and easy to untie, even when a line is under tension, by pushing forward the bight that encircles the standing part of the line. A major disadvantage is in its tendency to work loose if it is tied with stiff line.

The running bowline makes a noose that falls open as soon as the tension comes off the line. The left-handed bowline is less secure than the bowline itself and is best avoided.

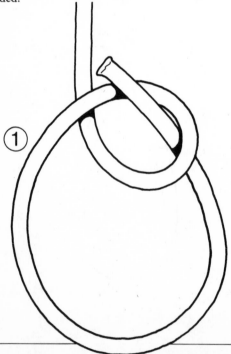

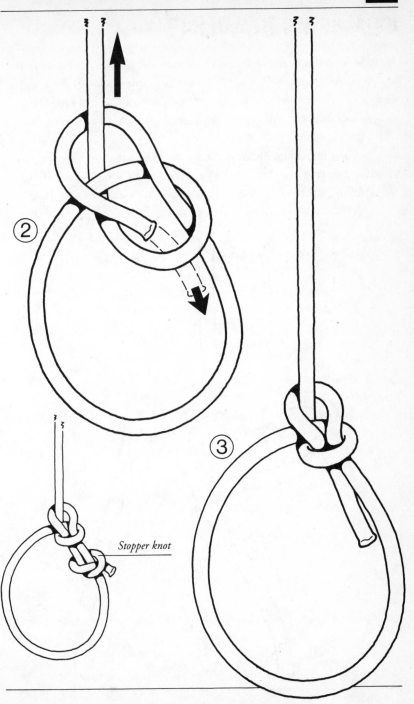

②

③

Stopper knot

CLIMBER'S BOWLINE

A climber's bowline is also known as a bulin knot. It is used as a safety measure during ascents when it is clipped into a carabiner. Climbers also tie this knot directly around their waists so they are able to adjust the length of line before undertaking an ascent. Whenever it is used in this way, it must be finished off with a stopper knot.

    A note of caution: Although the climber's bowline is fast to tie and easily untied, it does have a tendency to work loose, especially if the rope is stiff. It should always, therefore, be used in conjunction with a stopper knot.

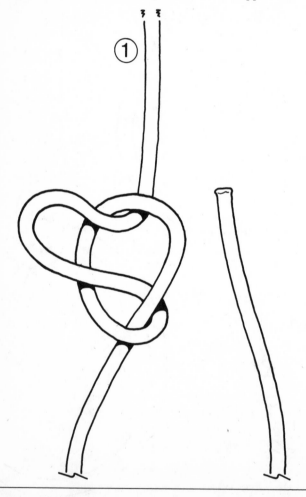

①

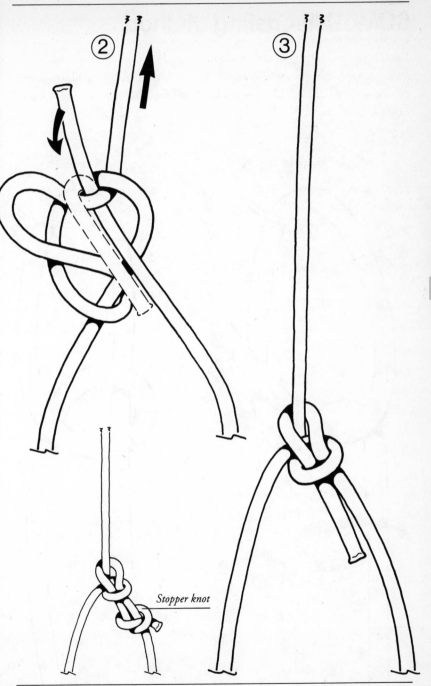

② ③

Stopper knot

BOWLINE Casting Method

Use this method of tying a bowline when you need to fasten a line around an object. Some synthetic rope might prove less reliable, so it is a good idea to secure the end with an extra half hitch, or to tuck it and trap it underneath one of the rope's strands.

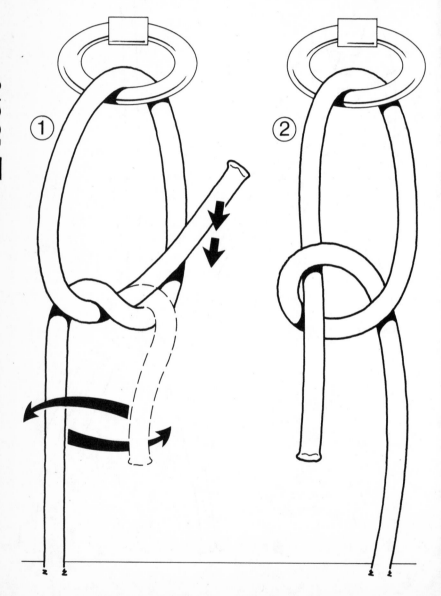

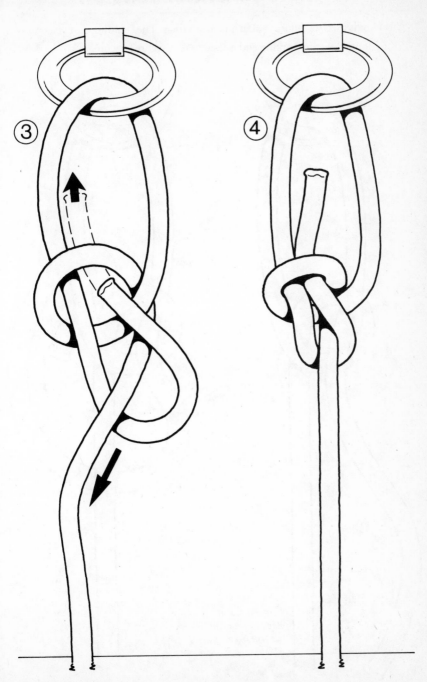

BOWLINE Rope Under Tension

This knot is used by sailors to attach boats to rings. The standing part stays taut throughout while the working end is used to tie a secure fastening.

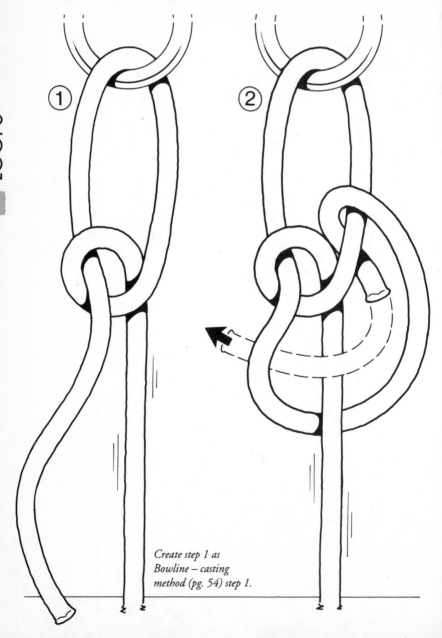

Create step 1 as Bowline – casting method (pg. 54) step 1.

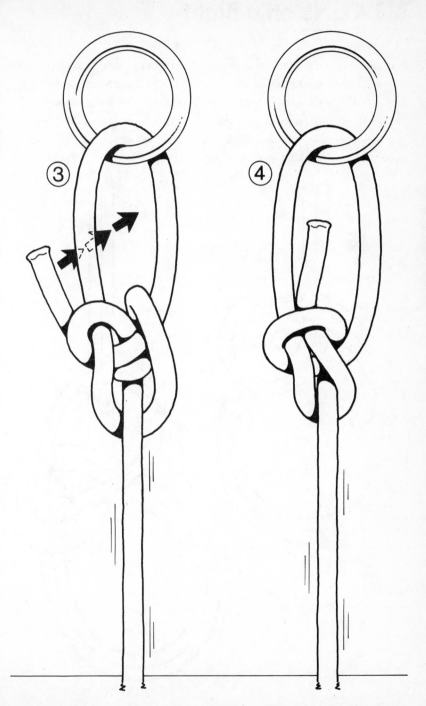

BOWLINE on a Bight

The bowline on a bight forms two fixed loops that do not slide. They are of the same diameter and overlap each other but, when opened out, they can be used separately. Although an ancient knot, it is still used today, especially in sea rescues. If the person to be rescued is conscious he or she puts a leg through each loop and holds on to the standing part. If the person is unconscious both legs are put through one loop and the other loop goes under the armpits. This knot is equally effective in salvaging objects.

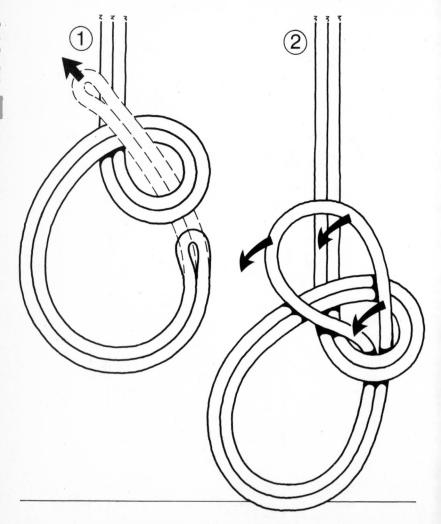

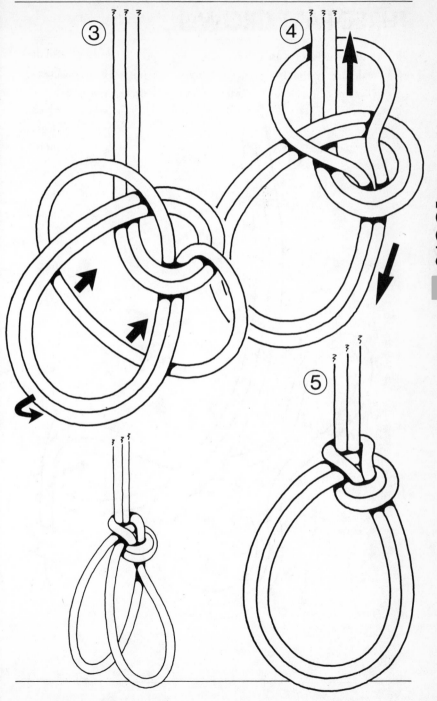

THREE-PART CROWN

This sturdy secure knot is used by campers to hang food and gear and it can be used as a decorative knot from which to hang objects. It is not generally used at sea as it becomes difficult to untie after it has supported a heavy weight.

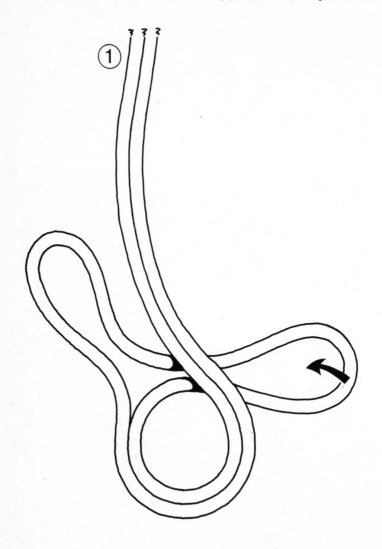

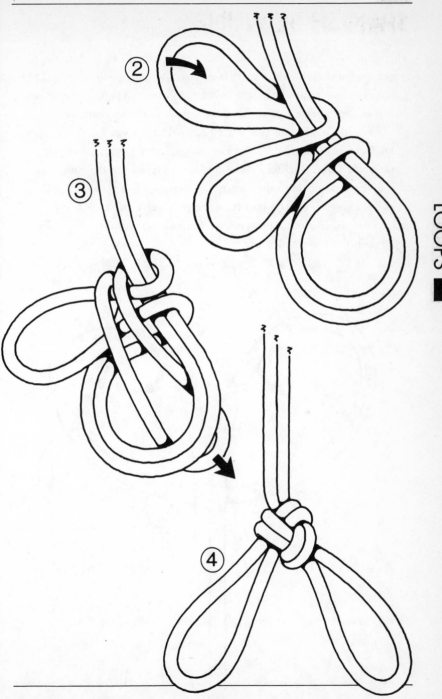

SPANISH BOWLINE

This is a very strong knot that is used widely in rescue work by fire brigades (when it is known as the chair knot), coastguards, and mountain rescuers. The Spanish bowline can also be used to hoist large objects in a horizontal position such as ladders, axles, even scaffolding if it is made in a heavy enough rope.

Like the bowline on a bight it is a very old knot, formed of two separate and independent loops that will hold securely and are very safe, even under considerable strain. To effect a rescue one loop is slipped over the casualty's head , around the back and under the armpits; the other loop goes around the legs behind the knees. It is vitally important that each loop is tightened to the individual's size and locked into position, otherwise an unconscious casualty could easily fall through the loops.

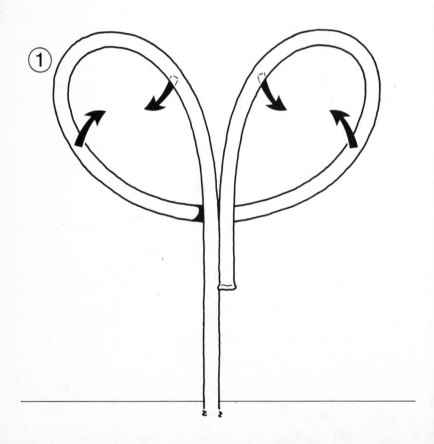

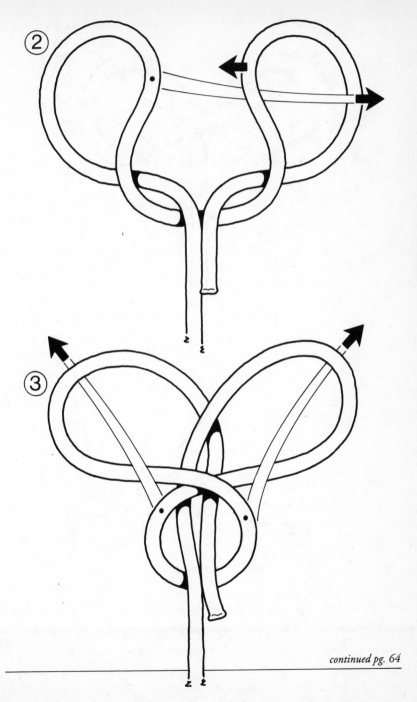

②

③

continued pg. 64

LOOPS

LOOPS

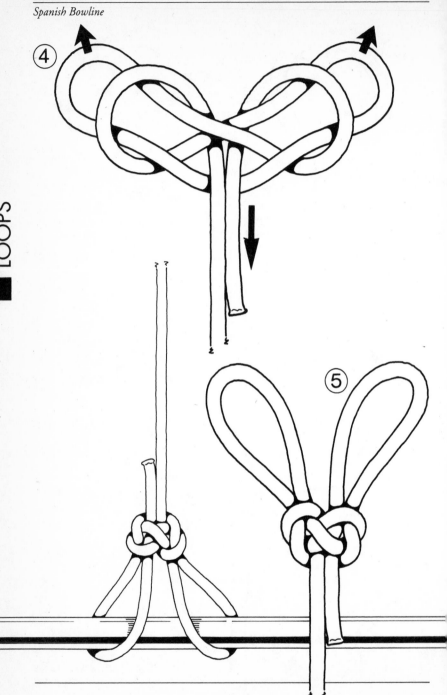

4
RUNNING KNOTS

Running knots, also known as slip knots or nooses, tighten around the objects on which they are tied but slacken when the strain is reduced. They are among the oldest knots known to man, having been used in prehistoric times to make weapons and trap animals. Hunters and poachers still use them today to make traps and snares. Campers and climbers use running knots to secure gear or when a rope may be subjected to heavy and sudden strain. One of the most famous, the hangman's or Jack Ketch's knot, has other, more sinister uses. They are not much used at sea, however, because of the way they slacken if not kept under constant strain.

This group of knots divides into two kinds: those formed by passing a bight through a fixed loop at the end of a line and those made from a closed bight knotted at the end of a line or along it. The main running knots in the first group are the noose and the running bowline; the hangman's knot and the tarbuck knot are the main knots in the second.

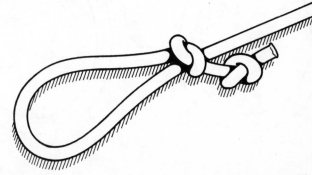

The Noose

RUNNING BOWLINE

This is probably the only running knot used by sailors; it is used on running rigging and to retrieve floating objects that have fallen overboard. On the old sailing ships this knot was used in high winds to tighten the square sail to the yardarm. It was also used by nineteenth- century poachers to make traps and snares.

The running bowline has many uses because it is strong and secure, does not weaken rope, is simple to untie, and slides easily. It is useful for hanging objects with ropes of unequal diameters – the weight of the object creates the tension that makes the knot grip.

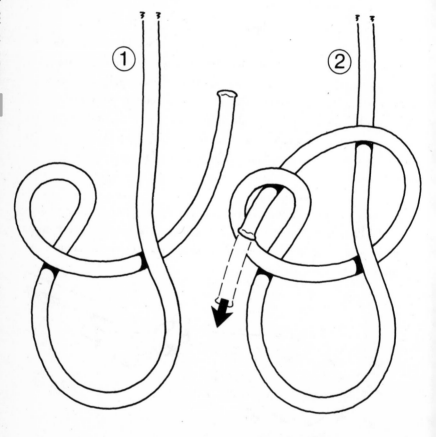

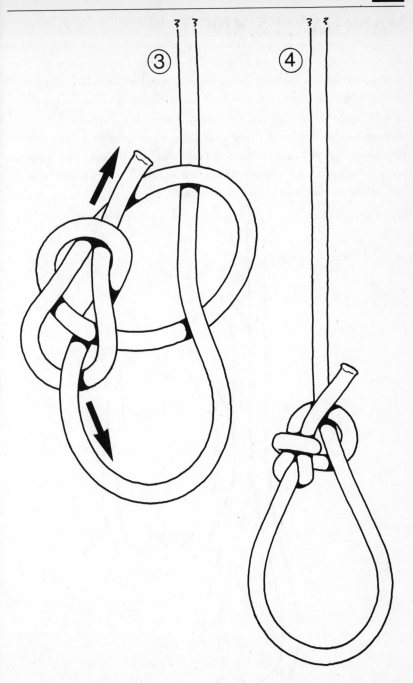

HANGMAN'S KNOT

This knot is one of the running knots made by knotting a closed bight at the end of the line. It forms a very strong noose that will withstand heavy jerks and shock loading. It slides without coming undone, but not always easily, so it is usually pre-adjusted to the required size. The name reveals its infamous use and the alternative name (Jack Ketch's knot) comes from the notorious hangman and executioner. Legend and superstition surround this knot. It was not, for example, permitted to tie it aboard ships of the British Royal Navy. It must always be tied with an odd number of turns between seven and thirteen.

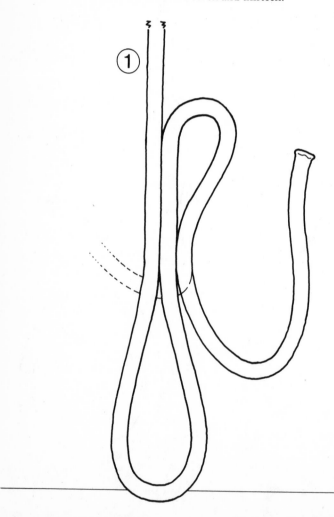

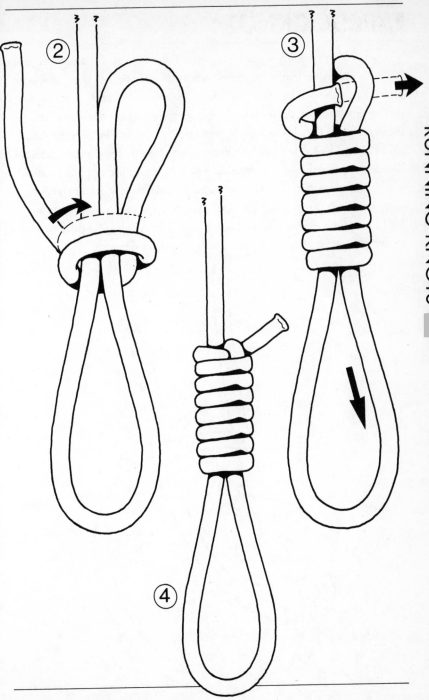

TARBUCK KNOT

The tarbuck knot belongs to the same group of running knots as the hangman's knot; it is formed by knotting a closed bight at the end of a line. It was developed for use by climbers when a line was likely to be subjected to heavy stress or sudden shock because the turns made in its formation enable the knot to absorb the strain. Since the advent of double braid (sheath-and-core) rope, it has fallen out of favor. These new ropes contain their own elasticity and the tarbuck knot's slide and grip action would damage the rope by stripping off the outer sheath.

It remains, however, a useful general purpose knot, which can be slid along the standing part and grips under strain. It is not particularly secure but it can be used for improvised tent guys, or a temporary mooring for small boats, or in any other situation where lives do not directly depend upon it.

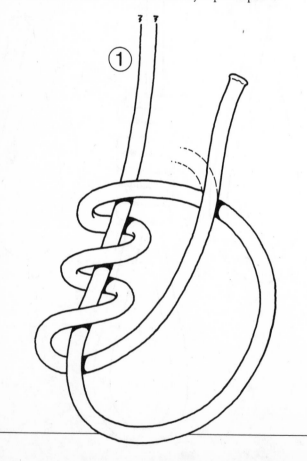

①

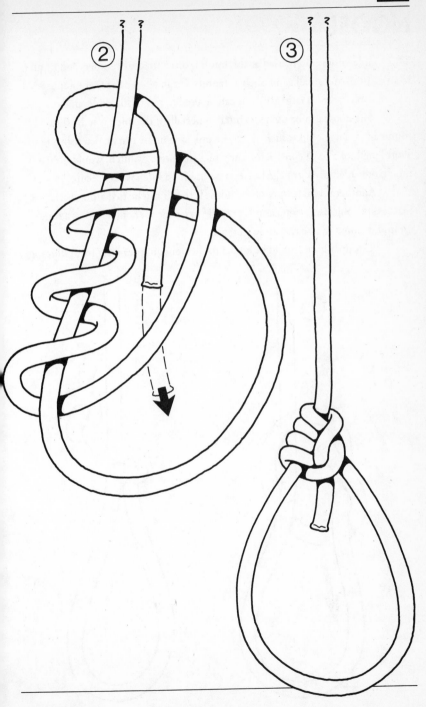

②

③

NOOSE

This simple knot is rarely used at sea, but it is often used by campers and hunters to snare birds and small game such as rabbits. It can also be the first knot used in tying a parcel or, on a larger scale, it can be used to put tackle cables under stress.

The noose can be used as a hitch, especially if the hitch is to be formed round a very large object, such as a tree trunk, as a noose can be tied using a fairly short length of line. A constrictor knot, or a clove or cow hitch, would need a much longer length of rope. Also, a noose used as a hitch is very secure.

Another useful feature of the noose is that it can be tied around relatively inaccessible objects. As long as it is possible to get close enough to pass a rope around, a noose can be tied and tightened.

A stopper knot should be added to the noose to prevent it from slipping.

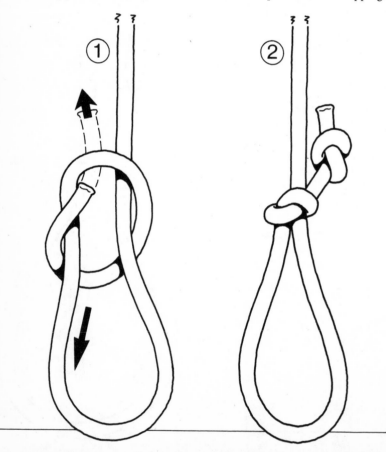

5
SHORTENINGS

Shortenings are invaluable knots, well worth mastering. As their name suggests, they are used to shorten lengths of rope or line without cutting. Rope is expensive and should not be cut unnecessarily. A rope shortened by means of knots can always be lengthened again at a later date, and a single unbroken line will always be more secure than two lines knotted together. Shortenings can be used to vary the length of a piece of rope to meet requirements. They can be used to tow cars, haul boats, load goods, put other rope under strain – in any situation where a short rope is needed. They are also a means of taking up worn or damaged lengths of rope. The weakened sections are incorporated into the knot and are not, therefore, subject to strain.

The most important shortenings are the sheepshank, used by sailors, and the loop knot, used by truck drivers.

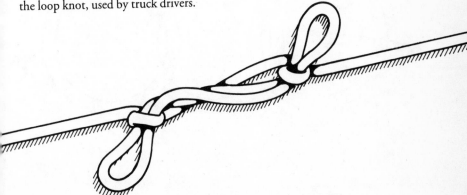

The Sheepshank

THE SHEEPSHANK

The sheepshank is very much a sailor's knot and shares the special characteristics of other nautical knots in that it does not chafe, it has a good jamming action, and it unties easily. It is easy to tie and holds under tension. It does not change shape, even if it has remained in place for a long time, and does not wear the rope (provided all the parts are under equal strain).

The sheepshank can be used to shorten any long rope to any required length without cutting. The number of half hitches made in the rope vary from three to five; they determine both the grip of the knot and the length by which the line will be shortened. In sailing the knot is used for towing boats and on running rigging but it has numerous other applications. It can be used to take up slack line and keep it out of the way, shorten guy ropes, and is well known to Boy Scouts. It is even used by bell ringers to keep their bell ropes tidy.

When a sheepshank is used to shorten damaged line, take care to ensure that the weakened section of the rope passes through both half hitches.

SHORTENINGS

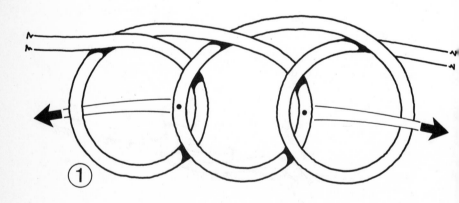

①

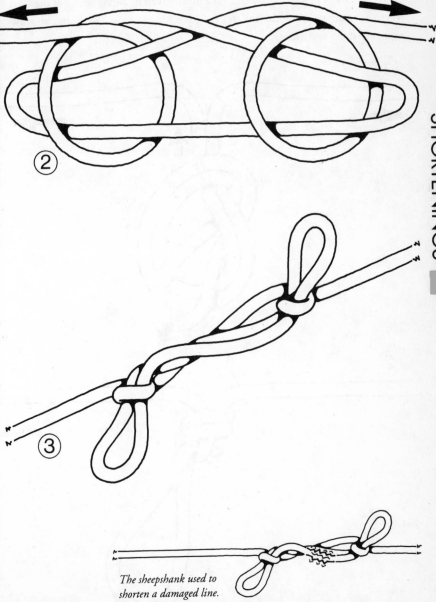

SHORTENINGS

② ③

The sheepshank used to
shorten a damaged line.

LOOP KNOT

This is a very simple knot but it is a vitally important way of shortening a damaged rope. The weakened part of the line is taken up in the center of the knot where it cannot be put under any strain. This knot is also used to shorten the tow ropes on trucks and cars.

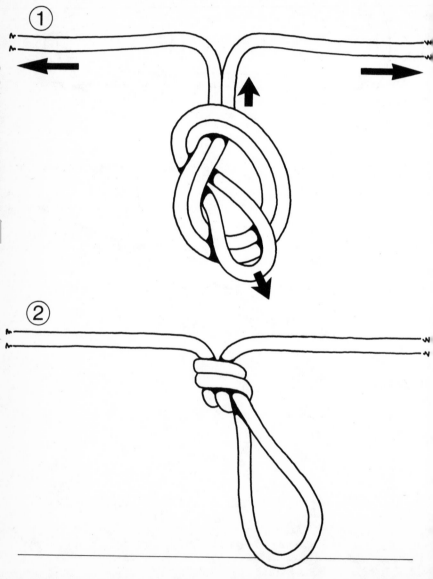

6
HITCHES

Hitches are knots used to secure a rope to another object (such as a post, hook, ring, spar, rail), or another rope that does not play any part in the actual tying. They are widely used in camping and climbing, and in sailing for mooring boats, fastening lines, and lashing. They have to be able to withstand parallel strain without slipping.

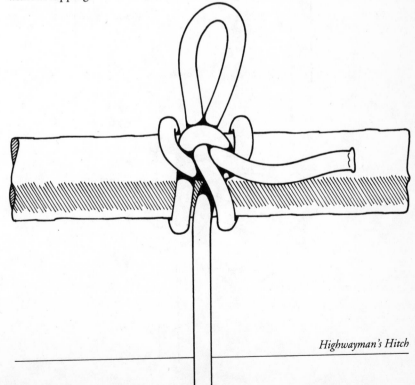

Highwayman's Hitch

HALF HITCHES

The half hitch is a very widely used fastening. It is, in fact, a single hitch formed around the standing part of another hitch. It is used to complete and strengthen other knots – as in the round turn and two half hitches – which can then be used for tying, hanging, hooking objects, etc. The slipped half hitch is a useful variation of the simple half hitch; a sharp pull on the end releases the knot.

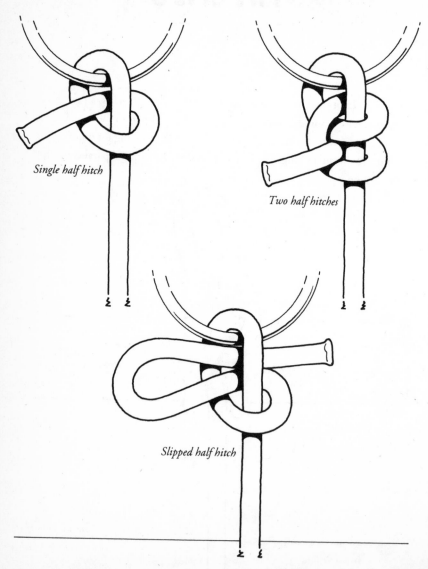

Single half hitch

Two half hitches

Slipped half hitch

COW HITCH

This hitch, also known as the lanyard hitch, is composed of two single hitches and is usually made on a ring or post. Often used for tethering animals, it is the least secure of all the hitches and should only be used as a temporary fastening.

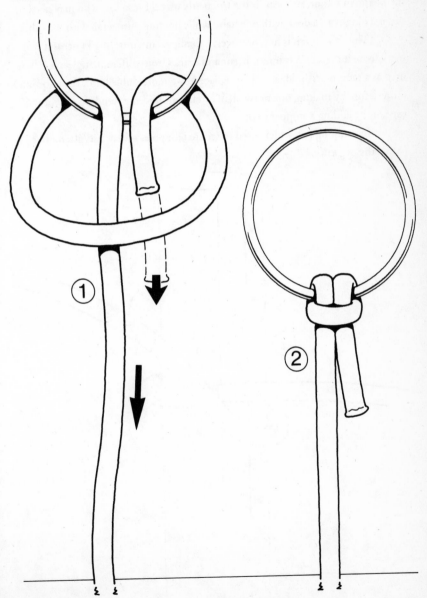

CLOVE HITCH

The clove hitch is one of the best known and most valuable of hitches. It can be used to fasten a line to a rail or post or onto another rope that is not part of the knot. It can, with practice, be tied with just one hand. As one of its other names, the boatman's knot, suggests, it is particularly useful for sailors who may need to moor a dinghy to a dock with one hand while holding onto a rail with the other.

The clove hitch is not, however, a totally secure mooring knot, as it will work loose if the strain is intermittent and comes from different angles. It is best used as a temporary hold, and then replaced by a more stable knot. It can be made more secure by making one or two half hitches around the standing part of the rope, or by adding a stopper knot.

In camping it is widely used to secure tent poles – hence its alternative name, the peg knot.

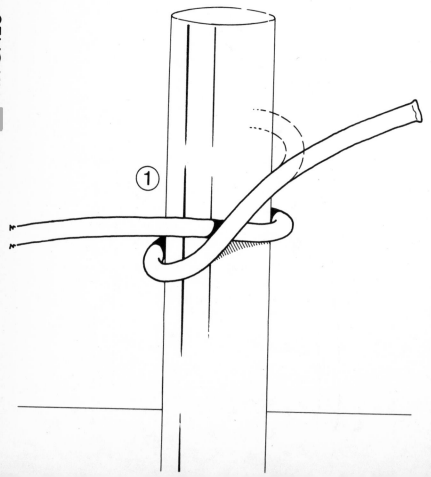

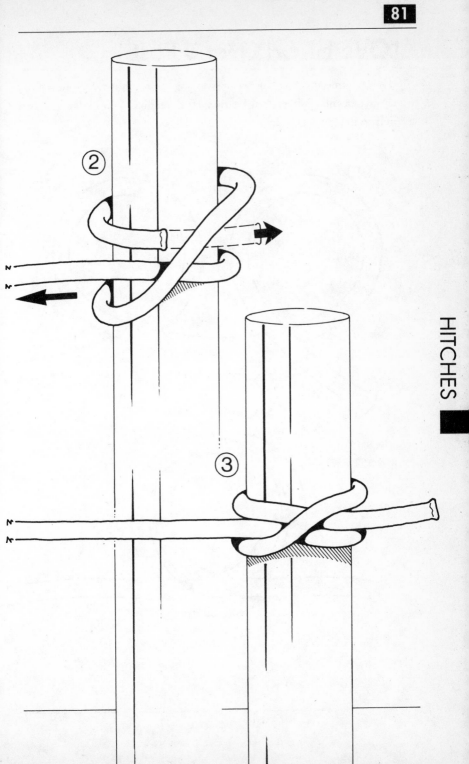

CLOVE HITCH Over a Post

The knot is formed by dropping two overlapping half hitches over a post. It is widely used in sailing for mooring boats to posts or pilings at docks. It is also used by campers to tighten guy ropes.

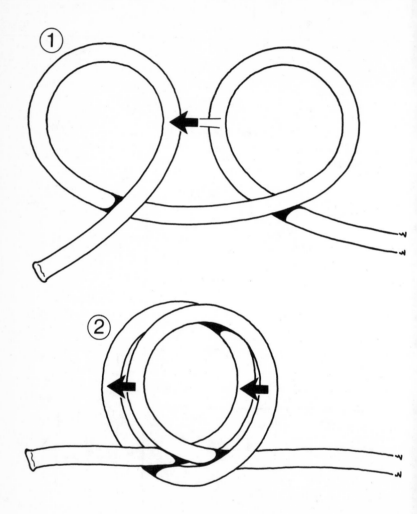

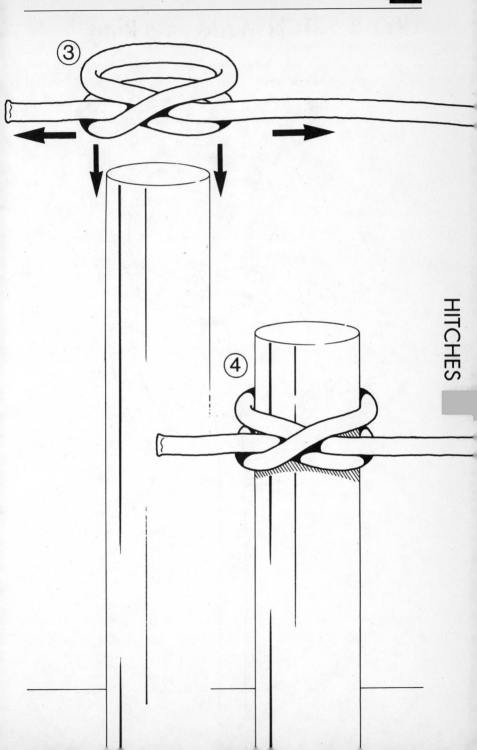

CLOVE HITCH Made on a Ring

This version is most commonly used in climbing and mountaineering, as it can regulate the length of rope between the climber and the piton (the spike driven into the rock or crack to support the rope). In sailing, where the ring is usually finer than the rope, the constant strain on the rope would cause dangerous chafing.

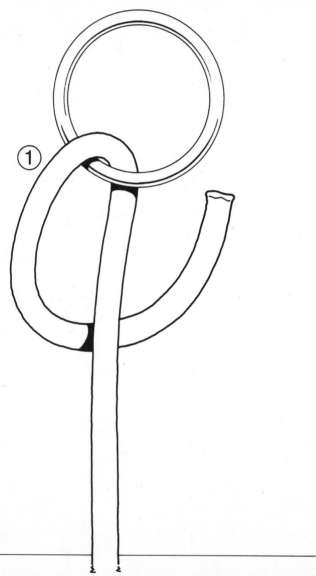

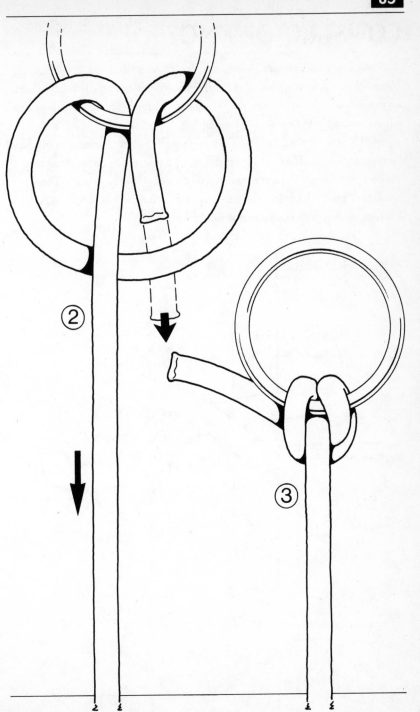

②

③

CONSTRICTOR KNOT

This is a popular all-purpose knot because it is firm and does not slip. It has dozens of uses. It can be used to secure the mouths of burlap sacks or fabric bags, on the ends of ropes as permanent or temporary whipping, and in woodworking to position and hold two pieces while glueing.

The knot is made by taking two turns with the rope, forming an overhand knot in the second. The left end is then threaded under the first turn, trapping the overhand knot under a crosswise turn that holds it firmly in place. The constrictor knot grips firmly and stays tied. It may have to be cut free unless the last tuck is made with a bight to make a slip knot.

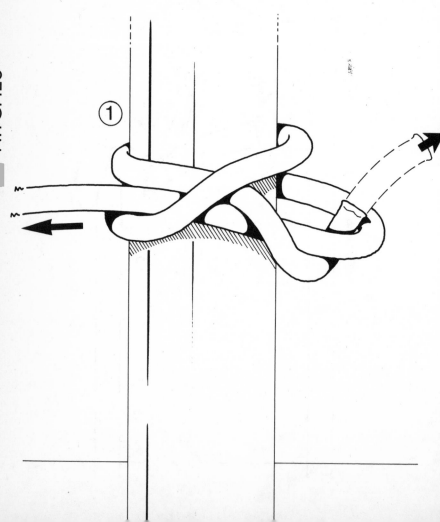

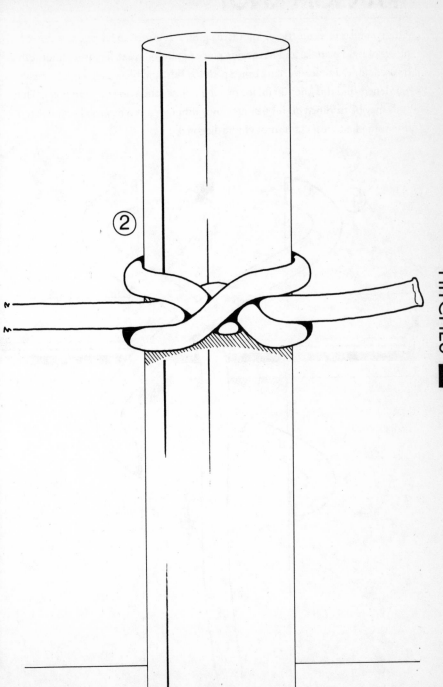

②

TRANSOM KNOT

This is similar to a constrictor knot (see pg, 86). It is used to fix together crossed pieces of rigid material and has a wide range of outdoor uses. Transom knots can be used, for example, to secure canoe paddles, skis, and bicycles to luggage racks. Gardeners find this knot useful for making trellises and tying up bean poles. The ends may be trimmed off for neatness and, although it can be prised undone, it is often simpler to just cut it through the diagonal.

HITCHES

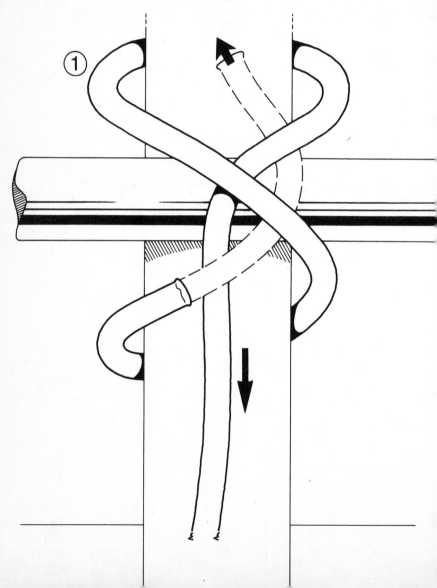

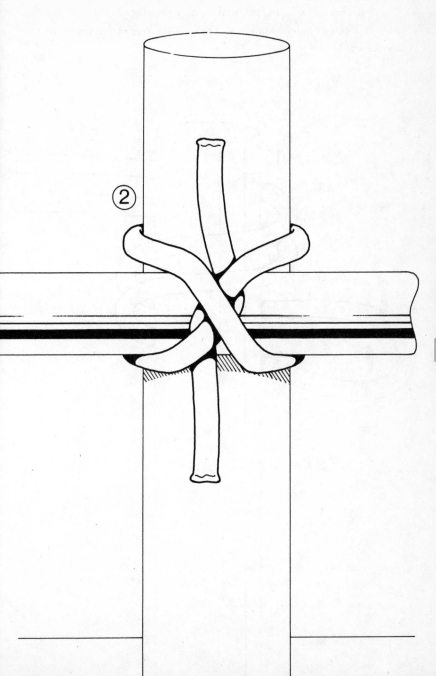

PILE HITCH

The pile hitch is a very neat and practical hitch for securing objects to a post –
ideal for a temporary mooring of a boat. The big advantage of this hitch is that it
is very quick to tie.

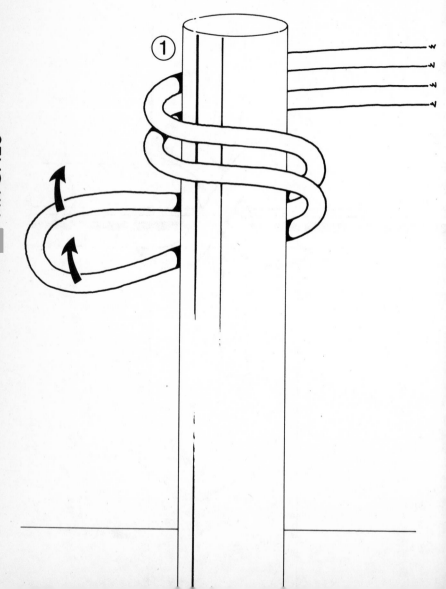

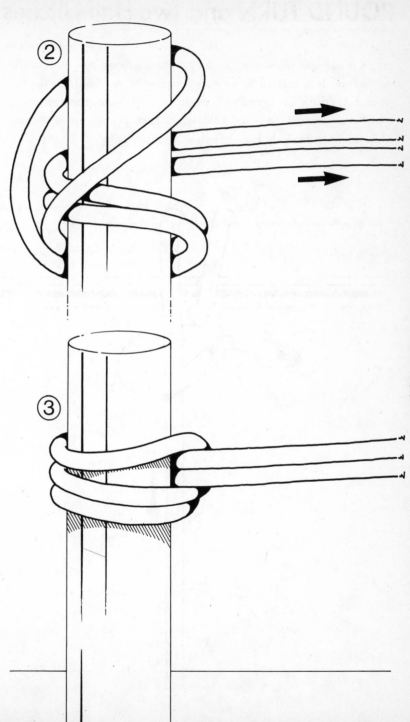

ROUND TURN and Two Half Hitches

This knot is strong, dependable, and never jams. This makes it very versatile; you can use it whenever you want to fasten a line to a ring, hook, post, pole, handle, rail, or beam. It moors boats safely and will support heavy loads. It has another advantage in that once one end has been secured with a round turn and two half hitches, the other end can be tied with a second knot. This is especially useful when fastening unwieldy, bulky objects onto car roof racks.

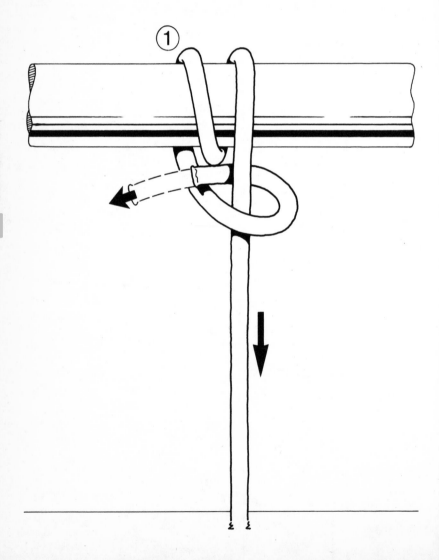

HITCHES

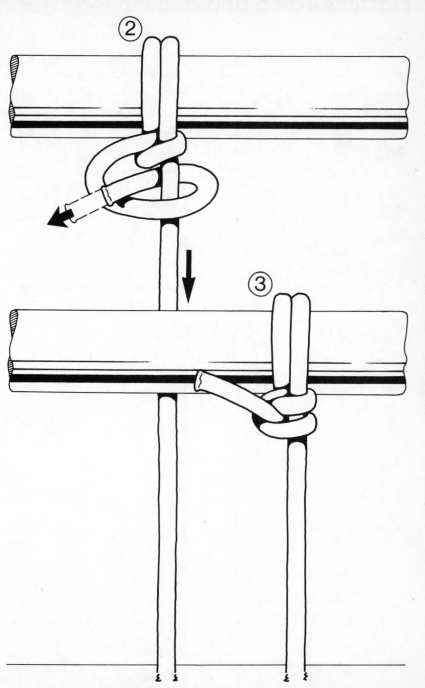

FISHERMAN'S BEND

The fisherman's bend is one of the most secure and widely used hitches. It is formed by making two turns around the post or through the ring and then tucking the working end through both turns. Adding a half hitch makes it extra secure.

It is used by sailors, to whom it is known as the anchor bend, to secure boats at the dock and also to tie onto the anchor ring. If it is used in this way, a stopper knot should be added for safety.

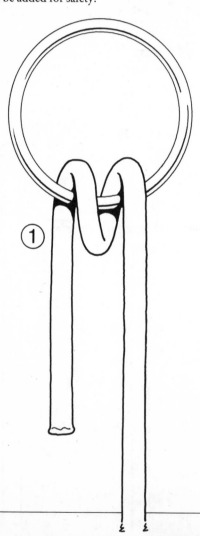

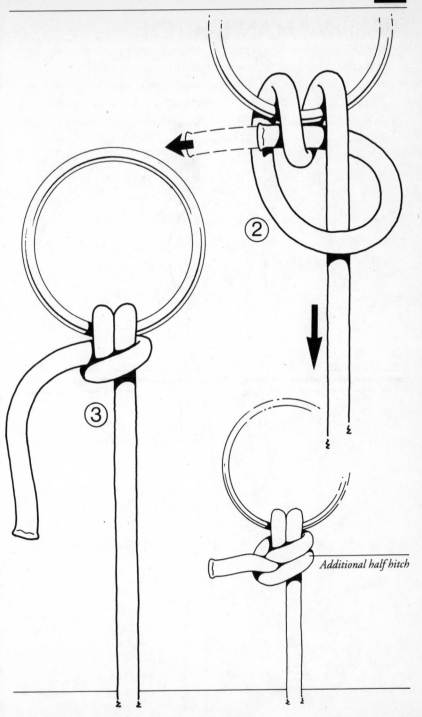

②

③

Additional half hitch

HIGHWAYMAN'S HITCH

The name of this knot comes from its legendary use by highwaymen and robbers to give them quick release of their horses' reins and so ensure a fast getaway. (It is also called the draw hitch). One pull on the working end and the knot is undone, but the standing end can be put under tension. It is useful for tethering animals, lowering loads, and as a temporary fastening.

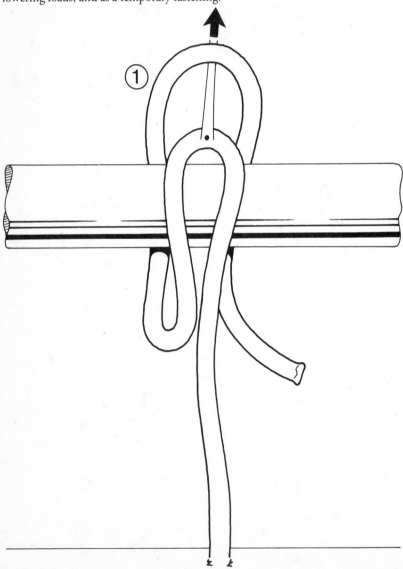

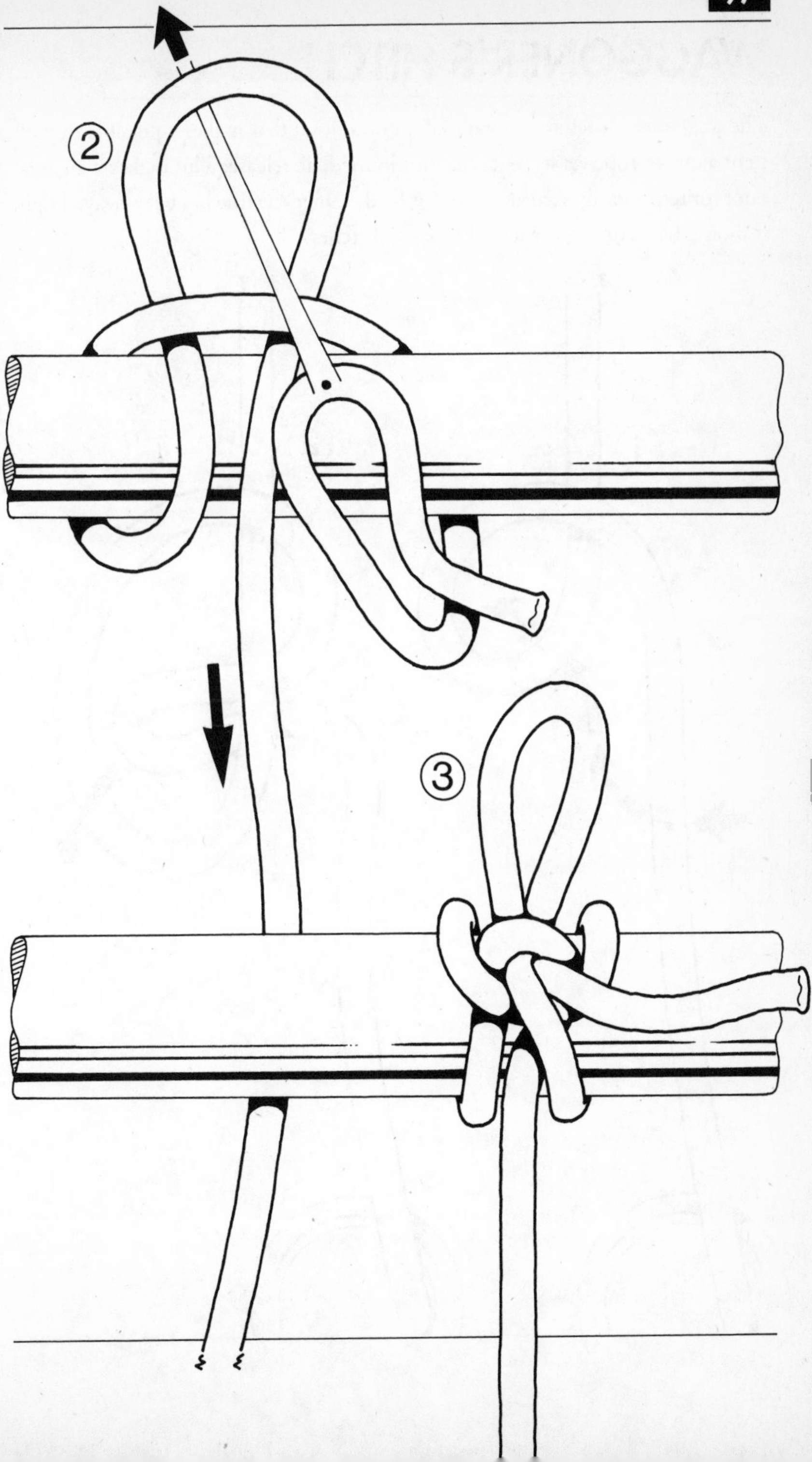
2
3

WAGGONER'S HITCH

The waggoner's hitch is a very useful outdoor knot that makes it possible to pull tight a line or rope yet leave it ready for immediate release. This makes it an ideal knot for temporarily securing items or loads. Once the line has been heaved tight it should be secured with at least two half hitches.

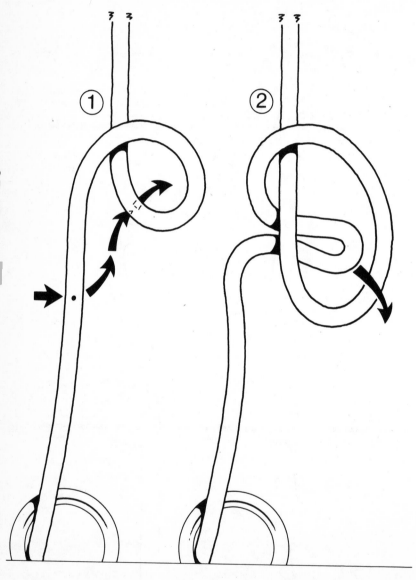

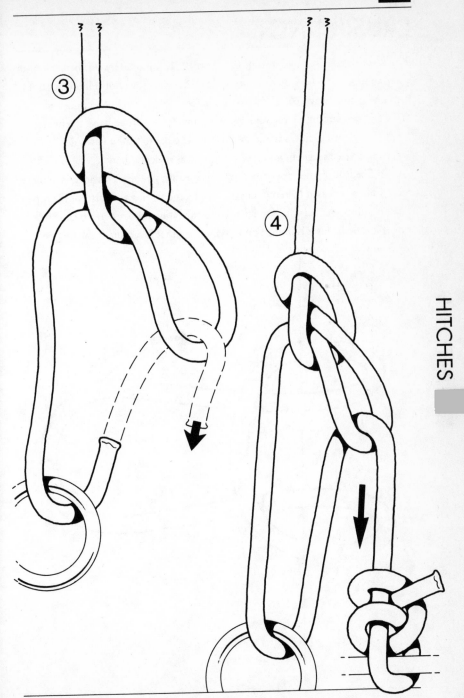

PRUSIK KNOT

This knot was devised by Dr. Carl Prusik in 1931. It is used by climbers to attach slings to rope in such a way that they slide freely when the knot is loose but hold firm under a sideways load. It is used as a safety mechanism in abseiling and rapelling (descending a steep rock face by using doubled rope fixed at a higher point). The Prusik knot is useful for anyone who has to scale awkward heights – for example, tree surgeons and cavers – as well as rock climbers.

The Prusik knot does not always slide easily and, once the load is in place, it can only be released by removing the weight and freeing the turns of the rope. The knot must be tied with rope that is considerably thinner than the line to which it is tied, and it is important to remember that it can slip if the rope is wet or icy.

HITCHES

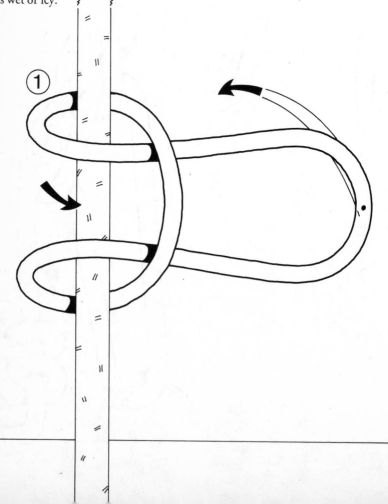

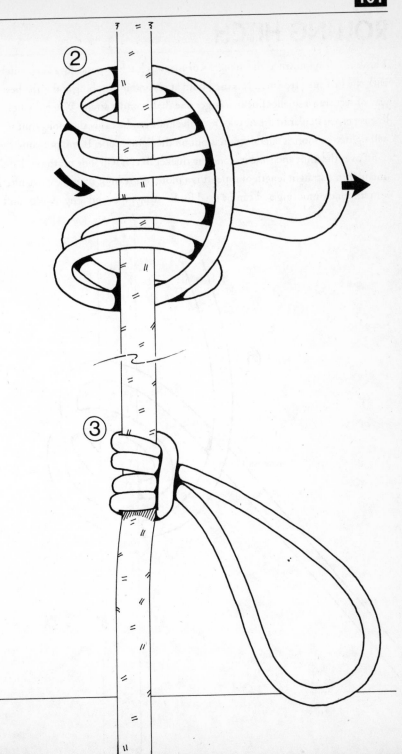

ROLLING HITCH

This knot, also known as the manger's or magnus hitch, is basically a clove hitch with the first turn repeated. It is used both at sea and in climbing and is the best way of securing a smaller line to a larger one that is under strain. When the lighter line is perpendicular to the heavier rope the knot can be easily slid along, but it will tighten as soon as lateral strain is put on the lighter rope. If you put your hand over the knot and slide it along the thicker line, it will slide off the end and uncoil into a straight length of rope. It is a more secure knot than the clove hitch for temporary mooring and can be used for hoisting pipes and long objects aloft.

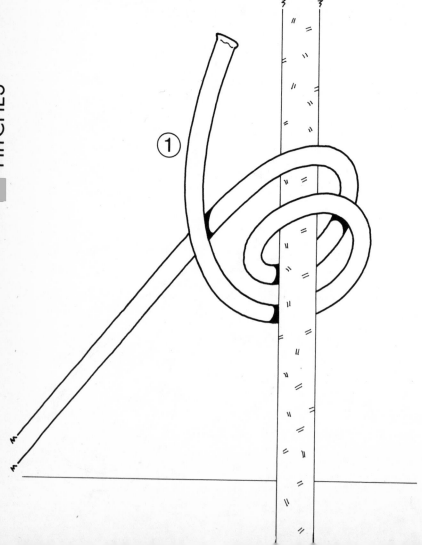

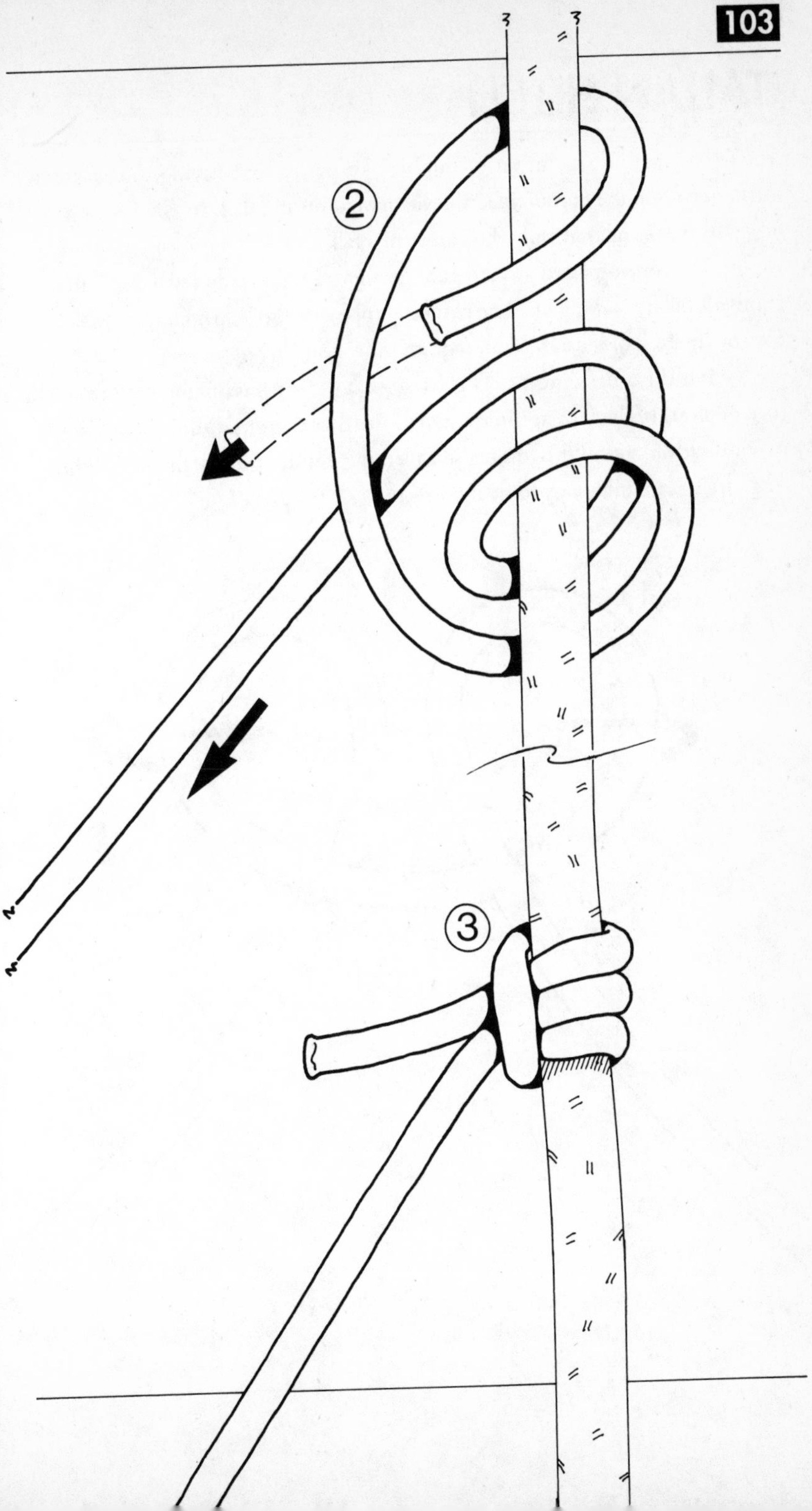
2
3

ITALIAN HITCH

The Italian hitch is an innovative climbing knot used for belaying, and was introduced into the mountaineers' lexicon of knots in 1974. Its chief advantage lies in its means of absorbing the energy of a fall.

The rope is passed around and through a carabiner and will check the climber's fall by locking up. The climbing rope can also be paid out or pulled in to provide slack or tension when required.

It is the official means of belaying (that is, fixing a running rope around a rock or cleat) of the Union Internationale des Associations d'Alpinisme. The major disadvantage of this knot, also called the munter friction hitch or sliding ring hitch, is that it is easy to tie incorrectly.

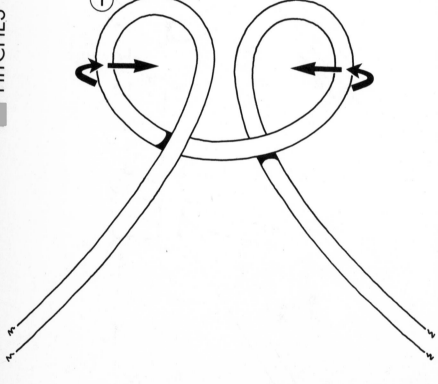

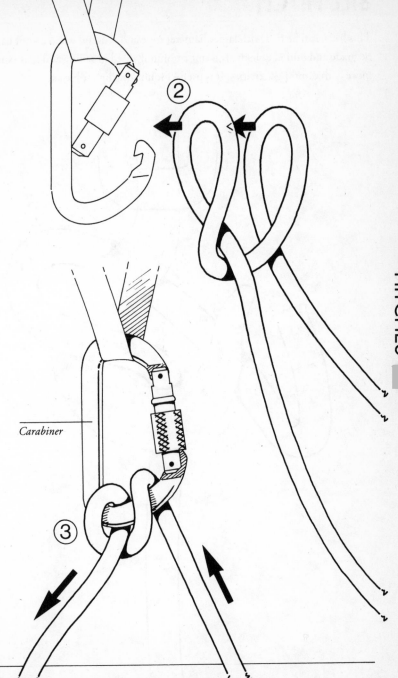

Carabiner

BILL HITCH

This hitch can be tied with large-diameter rope and is useful when a knot has to be made and untied quickly. It is not commonly used in sailing and is associated more with camping activities. It is useful for hoisting light objects.

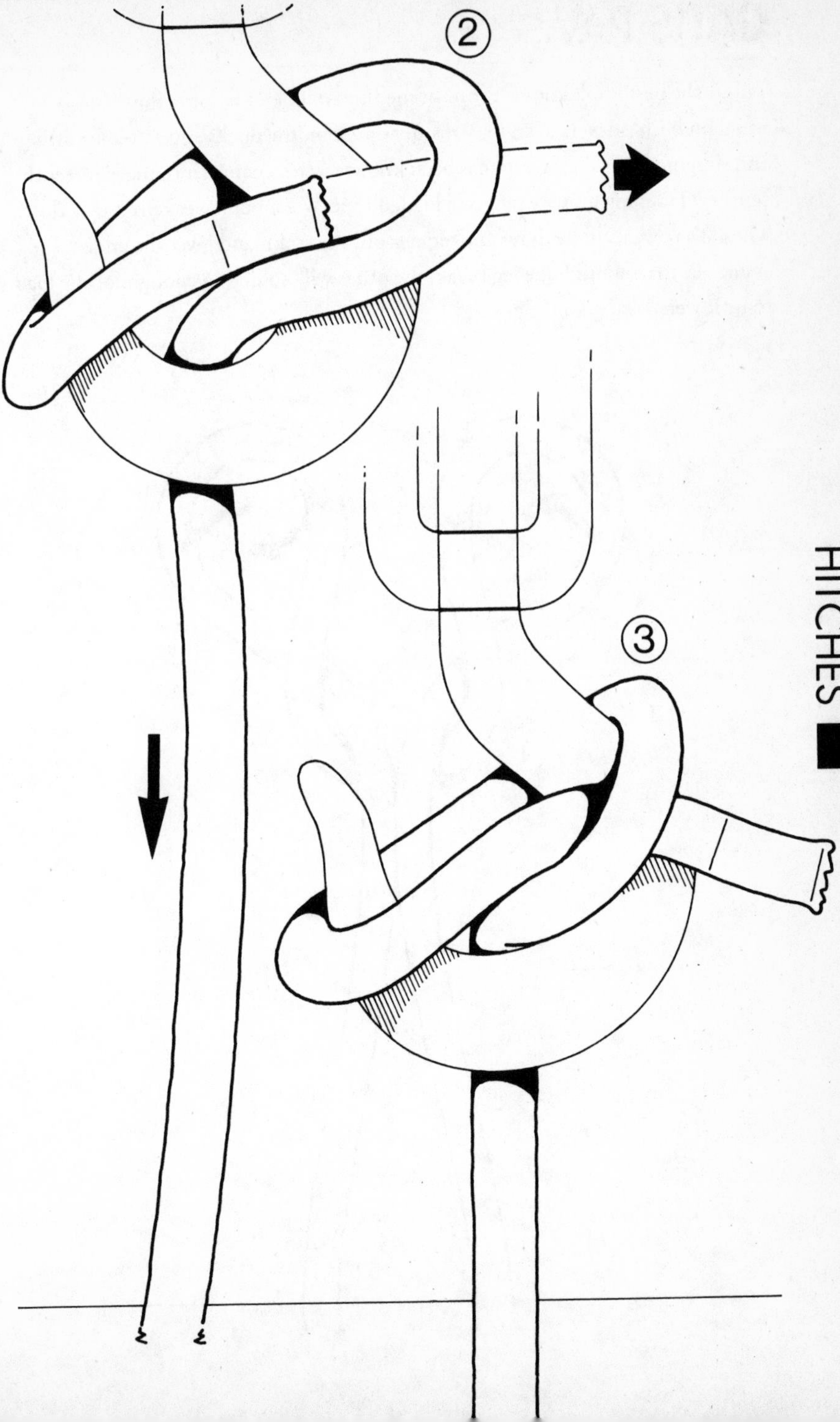
2
3

CAT'S PAW

This is the best hook knot for rope of medium diameter because the strain is equal on both sides. It has a long history of use on the docks and at sea for lifting and slinging heavy loads, and has been known by this name since the eighteenth century. Hanging a single part of a loaded rope over a hook weakens it by a third. The cat's paw, securely drawn up, equals out the strain and gives the added assurance that, should one leg break, the other will hold long enough for the load to be lowered safely to the ground.

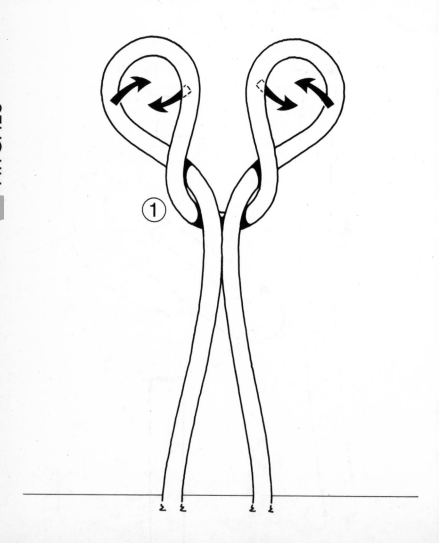

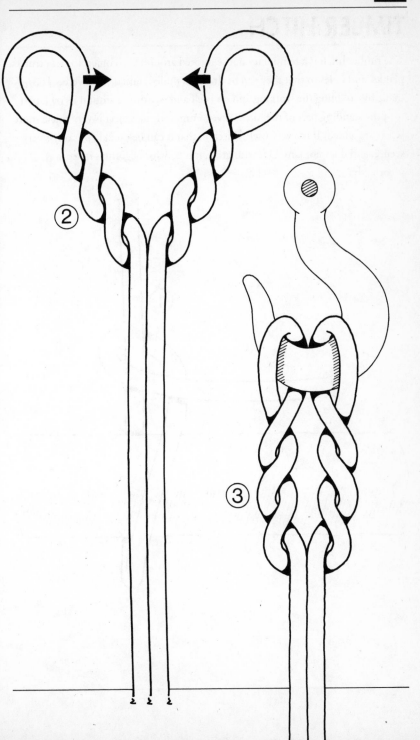

② ③

TIMBER HITCH

The timber hitch is a temporary noose formed around such objects as tree trunks, planks, and poles so that they can be dragged, pulled, raised, or lowered. It is made by doubling the working end on itself and twisting it around its own part (not the standing part of the hitch) several times. If the object is very thick, more twists are added. It is a very useful hitch in that it can be quickly put on, is very secure, and does not jam. Unfortunately, it is easy for beginners to tie it incorrectly.

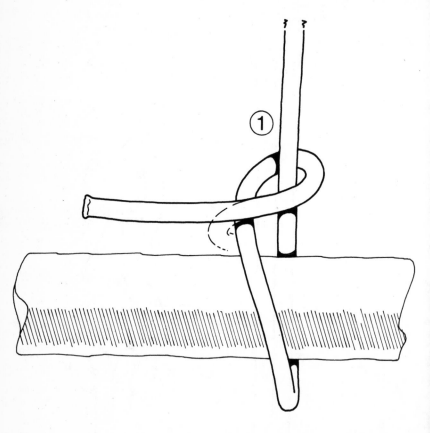

HITCHES

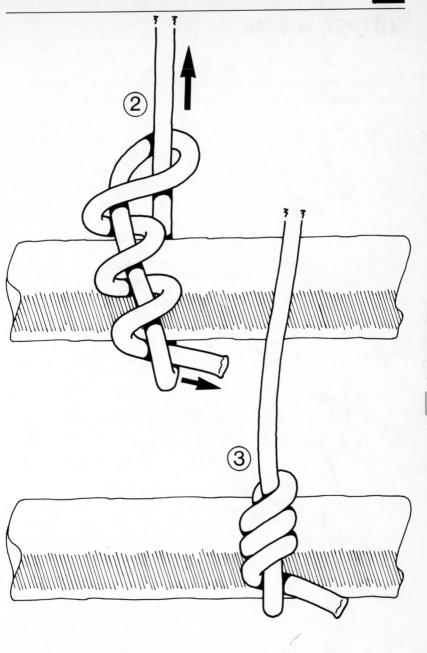

KILLICK HITCH

The killick hitch is a variation of the timber hitch specifically used for dragging and towing. It is created by first tying a timber hitch (pg.110) and then, some distance down the line, adding a half hitch.

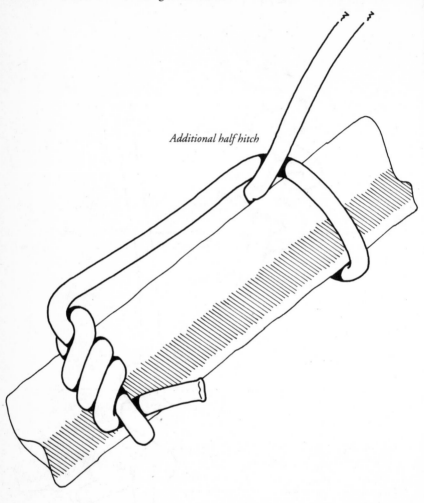

Additional half hitch

7
FISHING KNOTS

Fishing knots of one kind or another have been in use for thousands of years. Since ancient times and in all societies human beings have been devising ways of securing hooks to lines, so it is no wonder that there is such an array of knots designed for this purpose. They are the product of imagination, ingenuity, and the search for perfection, and although technically they can be classified in the ways already described (stopper knots, hitches, loops, etc.), they are not known by these names (to fishermen they are all knots), and they are not usually grouped according to the way they are formed but by their function.

Fishing knots are tied with fine monofilament line and the hooks they are tied to may be very tiny. Knots must be tied correctly and securely if they are to be of any use and tying them requires practice and considerable manual dexterity. A cold riverbank, in half light, and a pair of wet, freezing hands are not ideal when attempting to tie a particular knot for the first time. It makes sense, therefore, to practice at home until you have mastered each knot and have the confidence to tie it out in the field quickly and easily. There are any number of fishing knots but if you get to know the knots described in the following pages, you should have enough to cover most situations.

The knots used by fishermen differ significantly from those used by sailors, mountaineers, or campers. Monofilament is tough, strong, and flexible nylon line that comes in breaking strengths up to one hundred pounds, but because of this, once the knots are tied, it is not usually possible to undo them. They are also generally bulky, incorporating many wrapping turns; despite their bulk, the fineness of the line means that they remain streamlined and the wrapping turns increase their efficiency. Some knots are even claimed to be one hundred percent efficient – as strong as unknotted line.

Each of the knots a fisherman uses performs a different function, and what is perfect for one task may not serve for another. One knot may be used to tie two lines together, another to join the line to a leader, others to attach a hook, lure, sinker or swivel – as many as eight different knots may be required.

Lubricating a knot tied in monofilament, with water or saliva, helps to draw it up with the minimum of friction and to seat it securely. Do not use a chemical lubricant, such as silicone, as it may stay in the knot and increases the risk of slippage when the line is in use and the knot is put under tension. The tighter you can draw a knot the more force it can withstand before it slips. For this reason, especially with heavier monofilaments, it is a good idea to use a pair of pliers for the final drawing up. It is impossible to achieve the same degree of tightness by just using bare hands. The finer the gauge of line used to tie a knot, the easier it is to draw it up tight and seat it securely.

The diameter of line is also a factor to consider when deciding which knot to use. A knot that works well with fine monofilament may not draw up tight when used in heavier gauge line. A useful point to bear in mind, when tying two lines together, is that lines of the same brand will tie a more secure knot. This remains true whether the lines being joined are of the same or different diameters. Lines made by different manufacturers differ in degree of stiffness and this can affect the success of the knot.

When a knot has been pulled up and firmly seated the end should be trimmed at an angle of forty-five degrees and as close to the knot as possible. It is important that the tag end does not stick out; if it extends, it can get caught up on the hook or catch in weeds. Use a pair of nail clippers, scissors, cutting pliers, or a tool designed for the purpose to do this cutting. Do not be tempted to burn the tag end off; you could easily damage the knot and the line.

Knots differ in the way they behave when subjected to different kinds of strain. Some knots are very strong as long as the tension applied is constant, but any sudden jerking and they will fail. If you want to compare the performance of different knots, try this test. Ask a friend to hold the end of some lengths of line and, wearing a pair of gloves to protect your hands, pull on the other ends. Vary a steady pull with a jerking action and you can determine which knot is stronger under different types of strain.

DOUBLE LOOP KNOT

The double loop knot, or surgeon's loop, will not slip and can be tied very quickly. It is tied with a single length of line; otherwise it is tied in the same way as the surgeon's knot (see pg. 38).

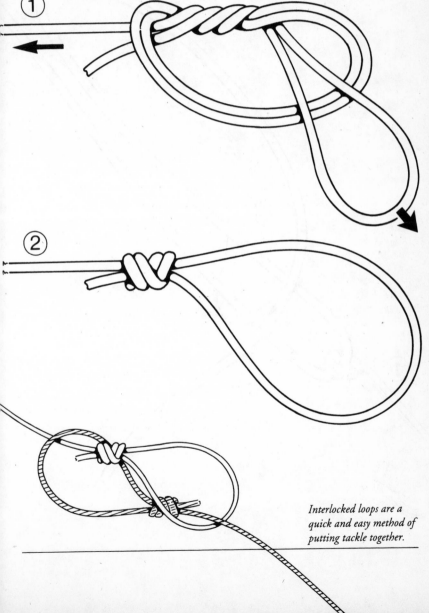

Interlocked loops are a quick and easy method of putting tackle together.

UNI-KNOT

This is one of the best and most popular knots for tying either a fly or an eyed hook to a leader or tippet. It is quite difficult to master, and is one of the knots a fly fisherman should practise at home. It's also called the Duncan loop or grinner knot.

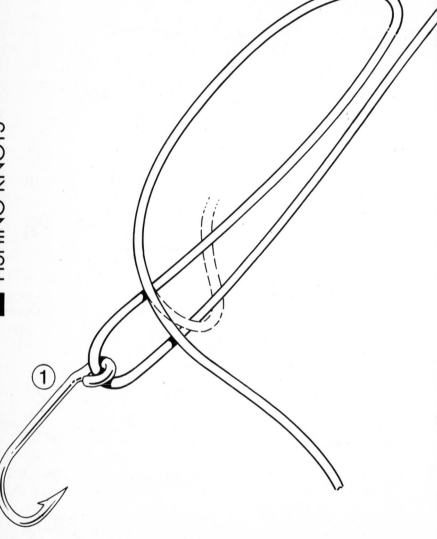

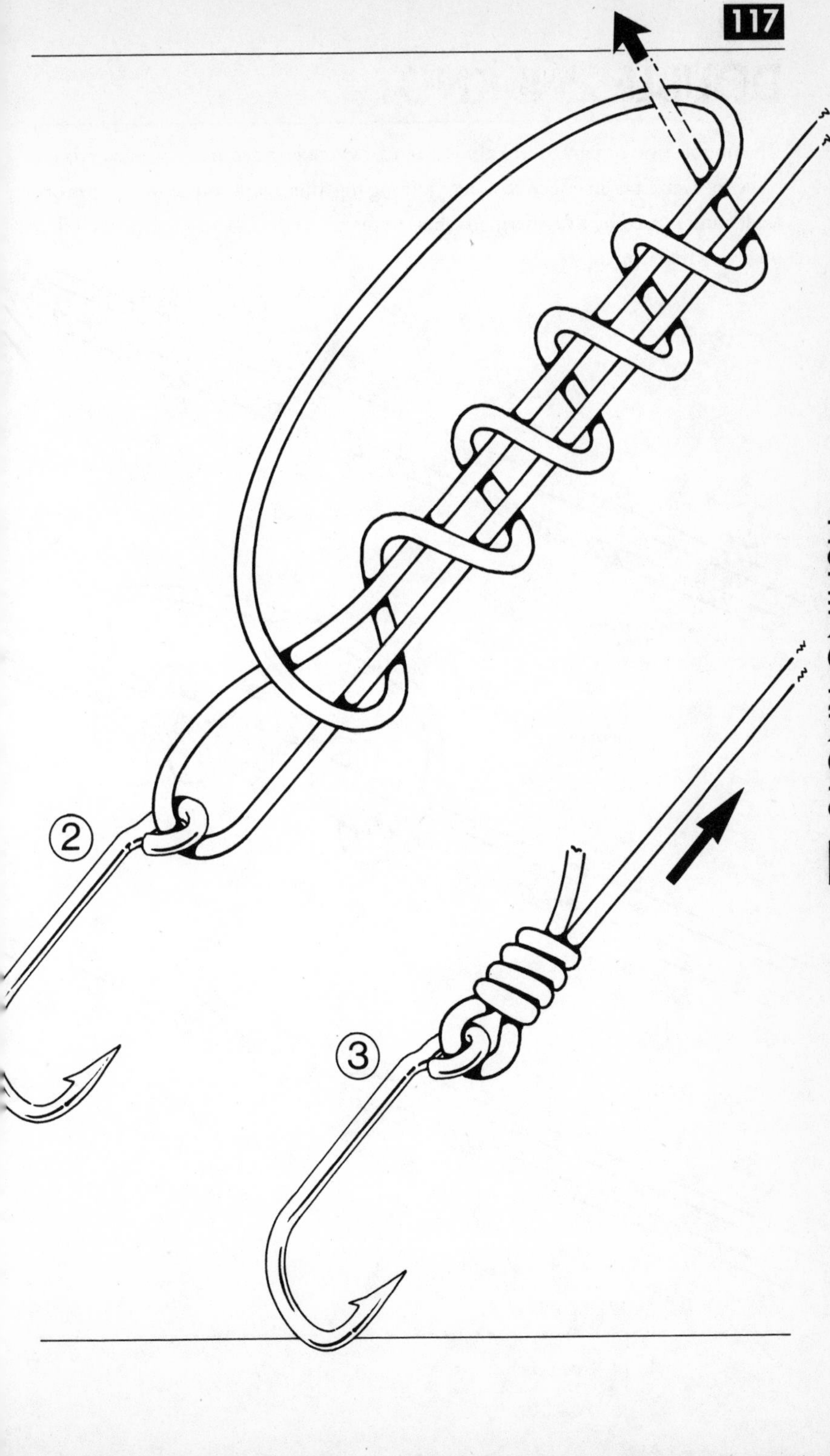
②
③

DOUBLE UNI-KNOT

The double uni, or paragum, knot is essentially two grinner or uni-knots tied back-to-back. It is an effective way of joining together two sections of a tippet or a leader and is used by fly fishermen when trying to catch large fish using small flies on a very fine tippet.

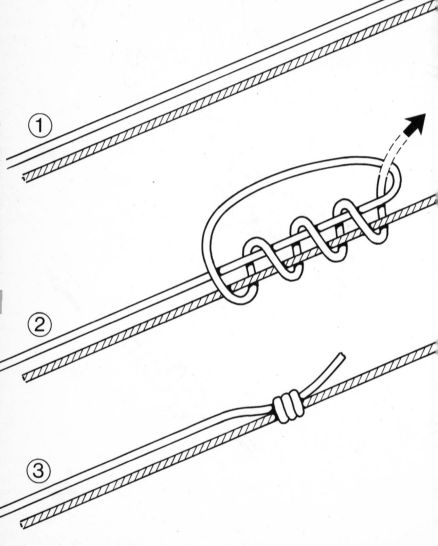

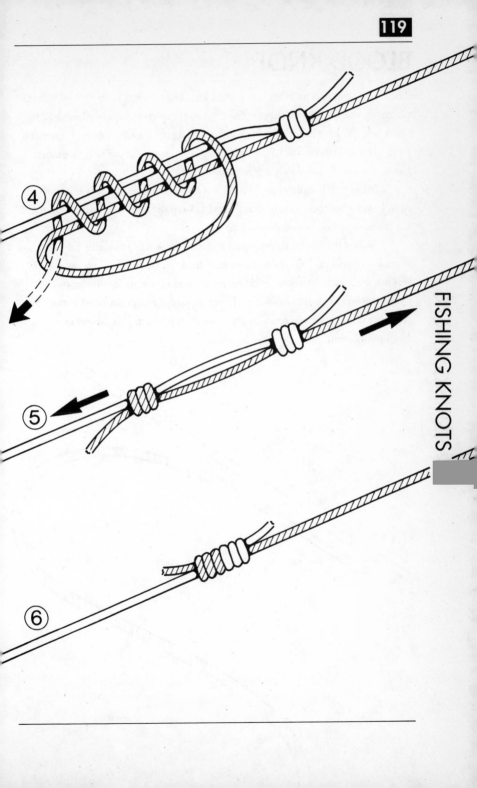

BLOOD KNOT

The blood knot gets its other name, the barrel knot, from the way it looks after the many wrapping turns that are required to complete it have been made. The turns help the knot absorb strain and shock and give it a relatively high breaking strain. It is used to tie fine nylon line of the same or similar diameter together; fishermen find it useful in many situations.

Although it looks complicated, it is not difficult to make. It is important to follow the number of turns exactly and to keep the knot loose while you make the turns so you do not confuse them.

When the knot is drawn up, it is almost impossible to untie. For many years, tackle makers kept the secret of how the knot was made to themselves. It was not until Jack Purvis, an engineer on an ocean liner, dissected the knot section by section and examined each section under a microscope, that the structure of the knot was revealed and passed on to the angling world in a 1910 publication.

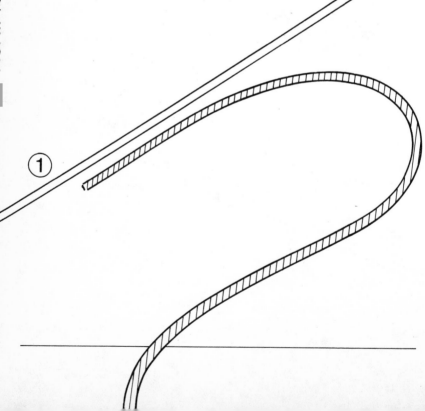

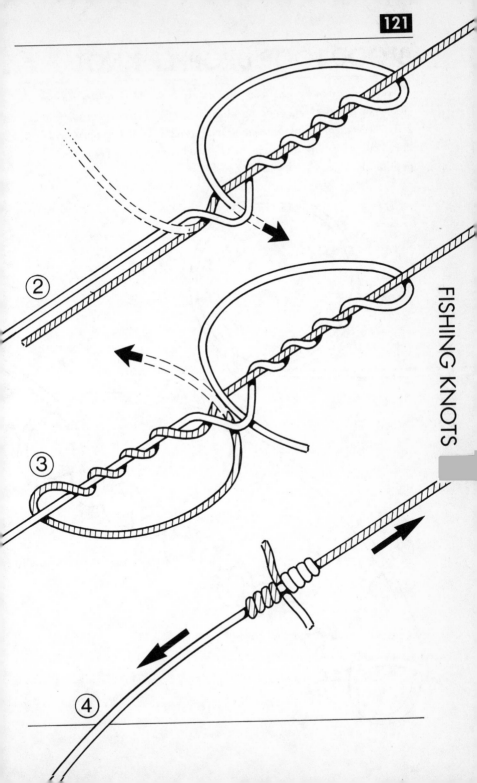

②

③

④

BLOOD LOOP DROPPER KNOT

This knot is used by fly fishermen when they want to add more flies to a line. The blood loop dropper knot, or dropper loop, is formed at right angles to the line and is an excellent means of attaching additional flies (called droppers) to a line, thus creating a paternoster system (a weighted line with a series of hooks positioned at intervals along it).

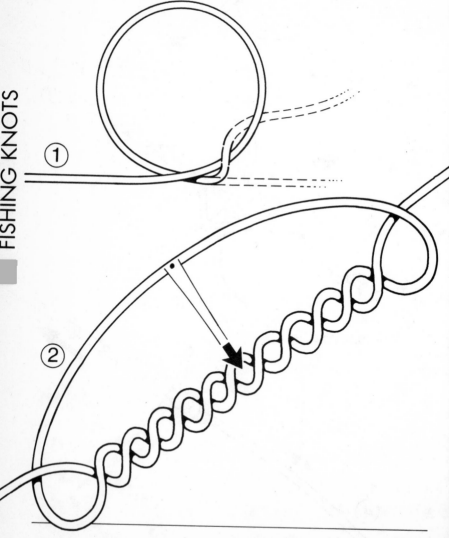

③

④

TUCKED HALF BLOOD KNOT

This knot is used by fishermen to attach a swivel, lure, or eyed hook to a line. It is an easy knot to learn and can be tied quickly, but it is not suitable for use with heavy line. To be really successful, it should be tied with fine monofilament. It is often called the clinch knot.

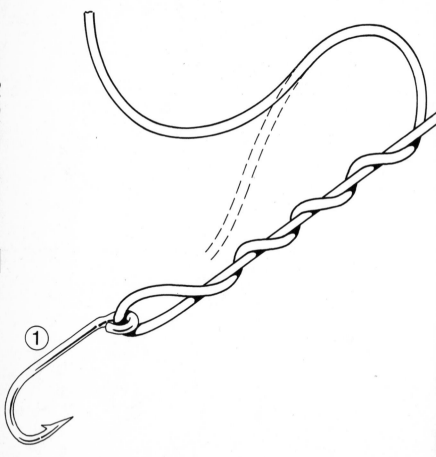

②

③

④

WATER KNOT

This very strong knot was first mentioned in print as early as 1496, and it was certainly known to Izaak Walton (1593-1683). Its excellent properties mean it is still very much in use today. It can be used to join lines of different diameter together, making it invaluable for attaching a leader to running line. The water, or cove, knot's already high breaking strength can be increased by simply tucking the ends three more times to create a quadruple overhand knot with both lines. These can then be drawn together in the same way as any other multiple overhand knot (see pg. 18).

①

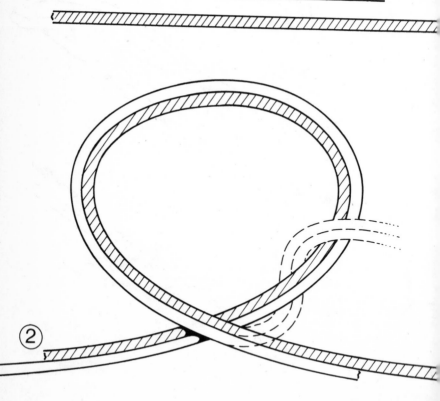

②

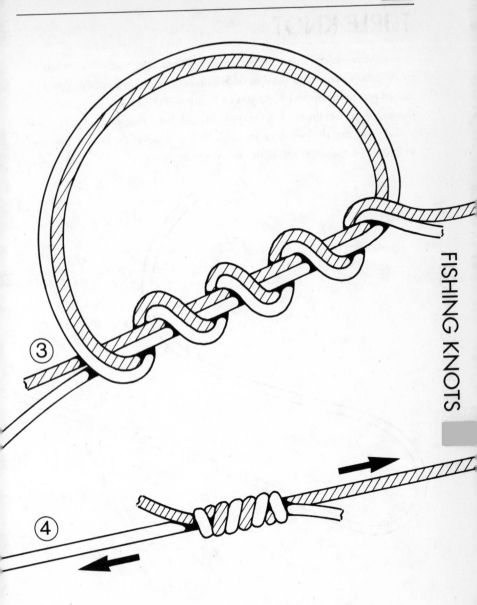

③

④

TURLE KNOT

Named after Major Turle of Newton Stacey, Devon, England, this knot is used by fishermen all over the world to tie flies on hooks with up-turned or down-turned eyes to the tippet (the narrow end section of the leader). Pass the line through the eye of the hook, form the knot, and then bring the hook up through it. Take care that the loop does not catch on the hackles of the fly and draw the knot tight on the upper side of the neck of the hook.

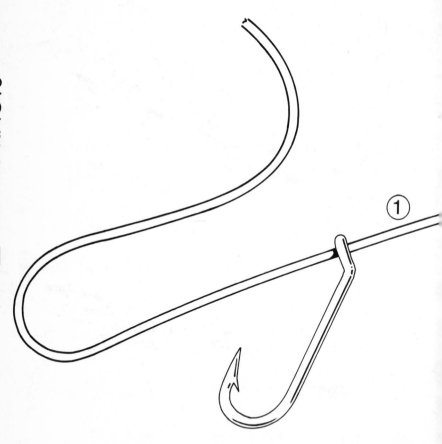

②

③

④

NEEDLE KNOT

The needle, or needle nail, knot is used to create a smooth joint between the fly line and the butt end (the thick part) of the leader. It is a very effective way of fastening monofilament to a fly line, as it is extremely strong and will not catch or snag in debris as it moves through the water.

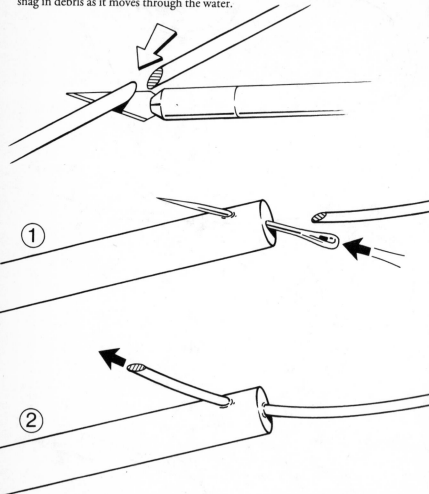

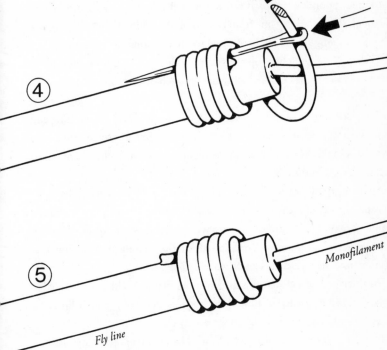

③

④

⑤

Monofilament

Fly line

GLOSSARY

Backing line. Monofilament or braided polyester line with a breaking strain of fifteen to thirty pounds or more. It is used under the fly line on a fly reel to bulk out the spool. It stops the fly line from twisting and forming tight coils and, if a big fish makes a long run, it can be allowed to run out after the fly line.

Bend. The action of tying two ropes together by their ends. It is the name given to the group of knots that are used to tie lines to each other or to some other object.

Bight. The slack section of rope between the working end and the standing end. The term is particularly used when this section of the rope is formed into a loop or turned back on itself. Knots tied "in the bight" or "on the bight" do not need the ends to be used in the tying process.

Breaking strength or **strain.** The manufacturer's estimate of the load that will cause a rope to part. This calculation is based on the strength of a dry line under a steady pull; it takes no account of wetness, wear and tear, knots, or shock loading. Lines are weaker when worn, wet, or knotted and the manufacturer's estimate cannot, therefore, be regarded as a safe working load.

Butt. The thick part of a leader. It is usually monofilament, although braided monofilament can be used. The butt of the leader is attached to the fly line.

Cable. A rope of large diameter: anchor warp or chain.

Cable-laid. Rope formed of three right-handed hawsers laid up left-handed to make a larger, nine-stranded rope or cable.

Capsize. The distortion that occurs in the shape of a knot when it loosens or slips under stress. Some knots are deliberately capsized to form another knot or as a way of tying or untying them.

Carabiner. A metal coupling link with a safety closure used by climbers and mountaineers.

Clear. The action of loosening tangled rope.

Cleat. A small piece of metal or wood with projecting ends on which rope can be fastened.

Cord. The name given to several tightly twisted yarns making a line with a diameter of less than one half inch.

Cordage. Collective name for ropes and cords, especially used to describe the ropes in a ship's rigging.

Core or **heart.** The heart or inner part, found in rope or sennet of more than three strands and in most braided lines, formed from a bundle of parallel strands or loosely twisted yarn and running the length of the rope. In some ropes the core acts as a strengthener or stiffener or gives the rope elasticity; in others it may just be there as cheap weak filler.

Dog. The winding back of the tail end of a rope around itself or around another (frequently larger) rope, with the lay, to secure it in a temporary way against a lengthwise pull.

Dogged. Whipping or sticking something through a draw loop to prevent it from accidentally coming undone.

Dropper. Short length of monofilament, with a wet fly attached, joined onto the leader between the fly line and the end fly. Some leaders are made by the manufacturer with droppers attached. Alternatively, droppers may be attached to a leader by means of a blood knot (see pg. 120). See **team of flies**, below.

Eight-plait. Strong, flexible line made from four pairs of strands, two spiraling clockwise, two spiraling counter clockwise. This kind of rope does not kink.

End. Generally the end of a length of rope that is being knotted – but see **standing end** and **working end**.

Eye. Loop formed at the end of a length of rope by splicing or seizing.

Fid. Tapered wooden pin used to work or loosen strands of a rope.

Foul. A rope that cannot slide freely because it is tangled or caught.

Fray. To unravel, especially the end, of a piece of rope.

Grommet or **grummet.** A ring, usually made of metal or twisted rope, that is used to fasten the edge of a sail to its stay, hold an oar in place, etc.

Hanger. See **pendant**.

Hawser. A rope or cable, five to twenty-four inches in circumference, large enough for towing or mooring.

Hitch. Knot made to secure a rope to a post, ring, spar, etc., or to another rope.

Kermantel. Modern synthetic rope made of an outer sheath of tightly braided fibers that fit over and around an inner core of filaments.

Lanyard. Short length of rope or cord, usually three-strand and often braided or made decorative, used to secure objects or rigging or as a handle for tools or personal gear.

Lay. The direction, right- or left-handed, of the twist in the strands that form a rope.

Lead. The direction the working end takes through a knot.

Leader. Thin, tapering length of nylon that forms the connection between a fly line and a fly. It may be tapered mechanically (thus knotless), or created by joining sections of line with reducing diameters. It is less bulky than the fly line itself, making delicate presentation of the fly possible. When floating line is used, lengthening the leader makes it possible to fish deeper water.

Line. Generic name for cordage with no specific purpose, although it can describe a particular use (clothes line, fishing line, etc.).

Loop. Part of a rope bent so that it comes together or crosses itself.

Marline. A thin line of two strands, often loosely twisted, used for whipping the ends of cables or ropes to keep them from fraying.

Marling. Lashing or binding with marline, taking a hitch at each turn.

Marlinspike or **marline spike** or **marling spike**. A pointed instrument, usually of iron, used to separate the strands of rope in marling or splicing.

Nip. The binding pressure within a knot that stops it from slipping.

Pendant or **hanger**. A short piece of rope with an eye spliced in one end and a hook in the other.

Plain-laid rope. Three-stranded rope laid (twisted) to the right.

Point. A tapered or decorative end of a rope used to help it reeve through eyes and holes.

Reeve. The act of threading or passing a rope through an aperture such as a ring, block or cleat.

Rope. Strong, thick cord more than one inch in circumference made from twisted strands of fiber, wire, leather strips, etc.

Safe working load (SWL). The estimated load that a rope will take without breaking, given age, wear and tear, knots used, and shock loading. The actual safe working load may be as little as one-sixth of the manufacturer's estimated breaking strength.

Seized. Fastened or attached by binding with turns of yarn.

Sennet or **sinnet.** Braided cordage (flat, round or square), formed from three to nine cords.

Slack. The part of the rope that is not under tension.

S-laid rope. Left-hand-laid rope.

Small stuff. Thin cordage, twine, string, rope, or line that has a circumference of less than one inch or a diameter of less than one half inch.

Splice. To join the ends of rope by interweaving the strands.

Standing end. The short area at the end of the standing part of the rope.

Standing part. The part of the rope that is fixed and under tension (as opposed to the free or working end, with which the knot is tied). In fishing, the standing part is wound around the reel.

Stopper. A short length of rope or chain used to check the running of a line or cable or hold lines while they are cleated.

Strand. Yarns twisted together in the opposite direction to the yarn itself. Rope made from strands (rope that is not braided) is called laid line.

Tag end. In fishing, the part of the line where the knot is tied. See working end.

Team of flies. Two, three or four flies attached to the same leader by short lengths of monofilament, or droppers. When three flies are used the top fly is known as the bob fly or top dropper, the middle is the middle dropper and the bottom is the point or tail fly.

Tippet or point. Thin, terminal section of the leader, to which the fly is tied. It is generally twelve to eighteen inches long.

Turn. One round of a rope. A turn is achieved by passing the working end around the standing part or a standing loop and is the basic element of the knot. To take a turn is to make a single turn with the rope around a cleat or post.

Warp. Moving a vessel from one place to another in a harbor by means of ropes or hawsers. Also rope or cable used for this purpose.

Whipping. Tightly wrapping small stuff around the end of rope to prevent it from fraying.

Working end. The part of the rope used actively in tying a knot. The opposite of the **standing end**.

Yarn. The basic element of a rope or cord formed from synthetic filaments or natural fibers.

Z-laid. Right-hand-laid rope.

ACTIVITY KNOTS

This section divides the most widely used outdoor knots shown in this book into five main activity categories. The first being a set of essential outdoor knots to cover most activities, and then followed by four specific sets of useful knots to know for camping, climbing, fishing and sailing.

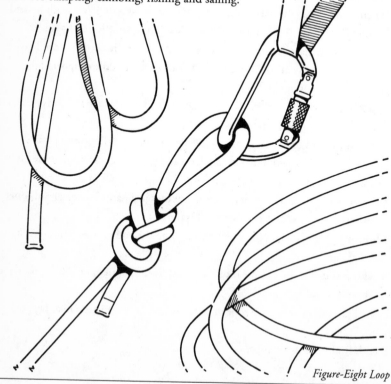

Figure-Eight Loop

ESSENTIAL OUTDOOR KNOTS

CAMPING KNOTS

ACTIVITY KNOTS

ACTIVITY KNOTS

CLIMBING KNOTS

FISHING KNOTS

SAILING KNOTS

INDEX OF KNOTS

. . . .

Personal Knot Notes

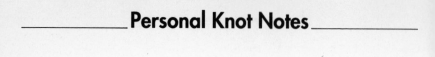